So schön ist/Beautiful

BONN

Ellert & Richter Verlag

Idylle mit Potenzial – So schön ist Bonn

In Bonn, so äußerte eine Freundin aus Berlin nach einem kurzen Stadtbummel durchaus positiv erstaunt, gingen die Uhren anders. Vor allem machte sie das fest an den zahlreichen Hannelore-Kohl-Frisuren, die sie heute noch in der Sternstraße gesehen habe. Tatsächlich: Wer täglich wie rund 30 000 andere Reisende aus dem Portal des kaiserzeitlichen Hauptbahnhofs wenige Stufen hinab förmlich in die Bonner Innenstadt hineinfällt, fühlt sich empfangen von der wohlhabenden Behaglichkeit der 1980er-Jahre. Die komplett fußläufige Innenstadt hat sich seither kaum verändert – sieht man davon ab, dass das Alte Rathaus jetzt in mutigem Zartrosa leuchtet. Große Kaufhäuser und Hunderte Spezialgeschäfte vom Sockenladen bis zur Comic-Börse, vom Puppenkönig bis zum Hut-Kontor säumen die Straßen, die nur zu sehr später Stunde nicht von Hunderten Flaneuren gefüllt sind. Traditionscafés servieren üppige Torten. Und Hausbrauereien gab es in der Stadt schon lange, bevor findige Werbestrategen Selbstgemachtes wieder zum Trend erklärten. Berlin mag hip sein, aber Bonn ist gemütlich, dem menschlichen Maß nicht entwachsen.

Idyll with potential – Beautiful Bonn

Very pleasantly surprised after a short stroll around Bonn, a friend from Berlin remarked that in this city time seemed to pass at a different pace. This judgement was prompted primarily by the number of women she had seen in Sternstrasse still sporting the type of hairstyle worn by Hannelore Kohl, wife of former Chancellor Helmut Kohl. It is true that when, as one of the 30,000 or so travellers who arrive each day, you exit through the portal of the imperial-era central station and walk down a few steps right into the city centre, you feel greeted by the comfortable affluence of the 1980s. This fully pedestrianised area has hardly changed since then – if you ignore the fact that the Altes Rathaus, or Old City Hall, is now resplendent in audacious pale pink. Large department stores and hundreds of specialist outlets selling everything from socks to comics, from toys to hats, line streets that are filled with hundreds of strollers until a very late hour. Traditional cafés serve sumptuous gateaux, and micro-breweries existed here long before clever advertising strategists declared that home-made was trendy. Berlin may be hip, but Bonn is cosy, having not yet outgrown human proportions.

Der Marktplatz ist die gute Stube der Stadt. Auf der Treppe des Alten Rathauses haben sich vor allem in der Zeit der „Bonner Republik“ viele berühmte Gäste dem Volk gezeigt.

The market square is the city’s “front parlour”. Especially in the days when Bonn was West Germany’s capital, many famous guests appeared in public on the steps leading up to the entrance of the Altes Rathaus (Old City Hall).

Bonn rangiert mit seinen gut 318 000 Einwohnern unter den 20 größten Städten in Deutschland. Im Zentrum merkt man das nicht. Noch immer prägen die Türme des Bonner Münsters (rechts) die Stadtlandschaft. Weiter hinten ragt der Posttower heraus, das größte Hochhaus Deutschlands außerhalb des Frankfurter Bankenviertels.

With more than 318,000 inhabitants, Bonn ranks as one of Germany's 20 largest cities. This is not evident in the city centre, where the towers of Bonn Minster (right) still dominate the urban landscape. Further back is the Post Tower, Germany's tallest high-rise building outside the Frankfurt banking district.

Zum Sonnenaufgang am Rheinpavillon am Anleger der kleinen Rhein-Fähre hat man das Flussufer noch für sich allein. Wenig später kommen Schulkinder und Geschäftsleute gleichermaßen mit der Rheinnixe über den Strom geschippert.

At sunrise by the Rhine Pavilion, near the terminal of the little Rheinnixe ("Rhine mermaid") ferry, you still have the riverbank to yourself. Before long it will be busy with both schoolchildren and business commuters who have crossed the river by ferry.

Idylle mit Potenzial – So schön ist Bonn

Über eine „kleine Hauptstadt für zwischendurch" spottete vor Jahrzehnten der Journalist Friedrich Küppersbusch und hatte – historisch betrachtet – ja durchaus recht. Andererseits wird es kaum gelingen, Menschen zu finden, die sich in Bonn nicht wohlfühlen und die der Stadt nach ihrem Abschied nicht die eine oder andere Träne nachweinen. Fragen Sie doch mal in der „Ständigen Vertretung" in Berlin nach, der rheinischen Kult-Kneipe in der Nähe des Regierungsviertels, auch wenn da längst andere Frisuren in Mode sind!

Dabei täuscht dieser erste Eindruck geflissentlich darüber hinweg, dass Bonn durchaus in der ersten Liga spielt. In der Rangordnung der Großstädte rangiert die Stadt am Rhein auf dem behaglichen Platz 19 zwischen Bielefeld und Münster. Geografisch betrachtet ist Bonn das Oberzentrum zwischen Köln und Koblenz im Schnittpunkt von Eifel, Westerwald und der Kölner Bucht. Drei internationale Flughäfen – Köln-Bonn, Düsseldorf und Frankfurt am Main – liegen in Reichweite, Autobahnen in alle Himmelsrichtungen, zwei Bahnverbindungen nach Norden und Süden und nicht

Idyll with potential – Beautiful Bonn

Decades ago, the journalist Friedrich Küppersbusch mocked it as a "small capital city for in-between times," and historically speaking he was absolutely right. On the other hand, it would be hard to find anyone who did not feel at ease in Bonn and who does not shed a tear of regret after leaving the city. Just ask people in the Ständige Vertretung, the popular Rhineland-style pub not far from the government district in Berlin, even though different hairstyles have long since been fashionable there!

Yet this initial impression conveniently ignores the fact that Bonn is definitely a premier-league city. In terms of size, the city on the Rhine ranks a comfortable nineteenth between Bielefeld and Münster. Geographically, Bonn is the main urban centre between Cologne and Koblenz at the intersection of the Eifel, the Westerwald and the Cologne Lowland. Three international airports – Cologne-Bonn, Düsseldorf and Frankfurt am Main – are within reach, along with autobahns in all directions and two rail connections to north and south, not forgetting Germany's busiest waterway – the Rhine. Two DAX-listed companies, Deutsche Post and

zu vergessen die meistbefahrene Wasserstraße der Republik – der Rhein. Die zwei DAX-Konzerne Deutsche Post und Telekom, fünf Hochschulen, eine Vielzahl an Dienstleistern, Behörden und wichtigen Organisationen sichern Stadt und Region überdurchschnittlichen Wohlstand und akademischen Background. Das macht Diskussionen über die Zukunft der Stadt zwar auf den ersten Blick nicht immer einfacher. Aber es sichert der Region im gesellschaftlichen und ökonomischen Wandel, bei der Verschiebung der Alterspyramide und der zunehmenden Digitalisierung der Wirtschaft eine Poleposition. Nichts hat diese These besser belegt als der Umzug von Regierung und Parlament. Ein Vierteljahrhundert nachdem die Möbelpacker in Richtung Spree abgezogen sind, geht es dem südlichen Rheinland heute besser als je zuvor. Und als – inoffizielle – zweite Hauptstadt und Hauptsitz der sechs Bundesministerien für Verteidigung, Bildung, Gesundheit, Landwirtschaft, Umwelt und Entwicklungszusammenarbeit prägt Bonn in wichtigen Fragen nachhaltiger Entwicklung fern des hektischen Berliner Parlamentsbetriebs die langfristige Politik.

Telekom, five universities, a large number of service providers, public authorities and major organisations secure the city's, and the region's, above-average prosperity and academic background. At first sight, that does not make discussions about the city's future any easier. However, it secures for the region a pole position in the midst of social and economic transformation, as the age pyramid shifts and the economy is increasingly digitised. Nothing substantiated this theory better than the move of government and parliament from Bonn to Berlin. A quarter of a century after the furniture removers departed for the city on the Spree, the southern Rhineland is doing better than ever before. And as Germany's – unofficial – second capital and headquarters of six Federal Ministries, for Defence, Education, Health, Agriculture, Environment and Development Cooperation, Bonn shapes long-term policy in key questions of sustainable development, far from the hectic parliamentary activity in Berlin.
One reason this works so well is probably that Bonn people have the image of a contented life constantly in view. Apart from a few inglorious exceptions, after 1945

Im Stadtteil Gronau ist das ehemalige Bundesviertel zu einem internationalen Bezirk mutiert. Heute prägt ihn der Campus der Vereinten Nationen. Bescheiden steht am Flussufer noch das kleine Wasserwerk, in dem 1991 der Bundestag den Umzug von Regierung und Parlament nach Berlin beschloss.

In Gronau, the former government district has been transformed into an international quarter dominated by the United Nations campus. Still standing unassumingly on the riverbank is the small Waterworks building where in 1991 the Bundestag resolved that the government and parliament should relocate to Berlin.

Das Rheinufer schafft viel Freizeitraum mitten in der Stadt – ob im Freizeitpark Rheinaue, dem Gelände der Bundesgartenschau von 1979 (oben links) mit dem Löffelwald (oben rechts) oder in Ramersdorf vor der alten Rohmühle (unten links) sowie im beliebten Biergarten am Alten Zoll (unten rechts).

The riverbank creates a great deal of leisure space in the middle of the city, be it in the Rheinaue Leisure Park, the site of the 1979 Federal Garden Show (above left) with its forest of spoons (above right) or in front of the old rawmill in Ramersdorf (below left) or in the popular beer garden by the Alter Zoll customs house (below right).

Das klappt wahrscheinlich auch deshalb so gut, weil die Bonner stets vor Augen haben, wie ein zufriedenes Leben aussehen kann. Bis auf wenige unrühmliche Ausnahmen wurde die stark zerstörte Stadt nach 1945 nicht im Brutalismus der 1950er- und 1960er-Jahre zugebaut. Zentrale Wegmarken blieben erhalten oder wurden liebevoll restauriert. Viele Straßenzüge atmen noch den Geist der wohlhabenden Rentiersstadt aus dem späten 19. Jahrhundert. Und die Tallage zwischen Venusberg im Westen und Ennert im Osten des Rheintals verhinderte die sonst üblichen monotonen Gewerbeparks. Stattdessen bietet die Topografie bis heute viel Grünraum mit dem weithin sichtbaren Siebengebirge, dem Kreuz-, Venus- und Godesberg, dem Kottenforst auf der Höhe, aber auch mit den von weitsichtigen Stadtplanern wieder angelegten Rheinauen. Hier in Bonn ist man nah dran an den Top-Ballungsräumen an Rhein und Ruhr, aber doch so erfrischend weit weg, dass man sich nicht ständig auf die Füße steigen muss.

the severely war-damaged city was not rebuilt in the brutalist architectural style of the 1950s and 1960s. Central landmarks were preserved or lovingly restored. Many streets still exude the spirit of the prosperous, late nineteenth-century city whose inhabitants lived on private means. Moreover, Bonn's valley location between the Venusberg hill to the west and the Ennert hills to the east of the Rhine Valley prevented the emergence of the dreary industrial park that is customary elsewhere. Instead, the topography still offers a great deal of greenery, with the Siebengebirge mountains visible from a distance, the Kreuzberg, Venusberg and Godesberg hills, the Kottenforst upland forest, along with the Rheinaue Leisure Park, laid out by far-sighted town planners. Here in Bonn you are close to the largest conurbations on Rhine and Ruhr but at the same time refreshingly far enough away not to be constantly treading on one another's toes.

Schloss Drachenburg liegt auf halber Höhe des Drachenfels vor Bonns Kulisse. Das Märchenschloss stammt aus dem 19. Jahrhundert und ist mit seinem gepflegten Garten und der tollen Aussicht unbedingt einen Besuch wert.

Drachenburg Castle stands halfway up the Drachenfels crag against the backdrop of Bonn. This fairy-tale castle dates from the nineteenth century and with its well-kept garden and stunning view is definitely worth a visit.

Vom Heerlager zur UN-Stadt – 2000 Jahre im Zeitraffer

Wer auf der vierspurigen Straßenschneise über Römerstraße und Sandkaule auf den Belderberg und weiter auf der B9 durchs linksrheinische Bonner Zentrum gen Süden fährt, der wird kaum ahnen, dass hier vor rund 2000 Jahren die Ursprünge der Stadt lagen. Zu Hauptstadtzeiten trug die Strecke den wenig rühmlichen Spitznamen „Diplomatenrennbahn". Botschaftsangehörige mit Diplomatenkennzeichen wurden damals nicht wegen Überschreitungen des Tempolimits belangt. Manche haben ihre Freiheit sichtbar genossen. Zwischen Nachkriegsbausünden hindurch fällt der Blick auf der Fahrt links immer wieder hinab zum Rheinufer. Es verläuft rund 15 Meter unterhalb der Straße. Der lang gestreckte Höhenzug, auf dem man unterwegs ist, wirkte nah zum Fluss und doch sicher vor dessen Überflutungen schon in vorchristlicher Zeit als unschlagbare Einladung für Häuslebauer. So war womöglich auch von ihm die Rede, wenn gallorömische Bewohner von *bonum* oder *bona* sprachen. Vielleicht war ursprünglich aber auch eine keltische Siedlungsgründung gemeint.

Es brauchte jedenfalls nicht erst den Glücksatlas der Deutschen Post, der den Rheinländern jüngst wieder

From army camp to UN city – Fast forward through 2,000 years

Driving south on the four-lane highway that leads via Römerstrasse and Sandkaule to the Belderberg and continuing along the B9 main road through the centre of Bonn on the left bank of the Rhine, you would hardly think that the city's origins lay here around 2,000 years ago. When Bonn was the capital of the Federal Republic of Germany, this route was disparagingly nicknamed "the diplomats' racetrack." In those days embassy staff with diplomatic number plates were not prosecuted for breaking the speed limit. Some visibly enjoyed their freedom. Driving along, between architectural blunders of the post-war era you catch repeated glimpses of the Rhine bank, which runs around 15 metres beneath the road. The ridge along which you are travelling is close to the river and yet safe from flooding, which made it a highly inviting location for house builders, even in pre-Christian times. This may be what Gallo-Roman residents were referring to when they spoke of *bonum* or *bona*. Or perhaps it was originally a Celtic settlement.

A recent "Atlas of Happiness" published by Deutsche Post again attributed Rhinelanders with especially high levels of satisfaction. However, there was no need of such

Die Römer legten mit einem Heerlager und einer zivilen Siedlung das Fundament für Bonns Stadtentwicklung. An der Münsterbasilika oder in der Heerstraße mit ihren Abgüssen römischer Grabmale haben sie Spuren hinterlassen. Und manchmal posieren Freizeit-Legionäre sogar am Rheinufer.

The Romans built the army camp and civil settlement that were the foundation for Bonn's development as a city. They have left traces by the Minster basilica and in Heerstrasse with its casts of Roman gravestones. Sometimes you can even see amateur legionaries posing on the bank of the Rhine.

besonders hohe Zufriedenheitswerte attestierte, damit sich die Attraktivität der Region herumsprach. Schon vor 14 000 Jahren genossen erste Menschen nachweislich die abwechslungsreiche Gegend. Darunter waren auch ein 50 Jahre alter Mann und eine kaum halb so alte Frau, über deren Beziehungsstatus sich Jahrtausende später mancher das Maul zerreißt. Jedenfalls tauchte das ungleiche Paar zusammen mit seinem Hund 1914 bei Steinbrucharbeiten im rechtsrheinischen Oberkassel aus einem gemeinsamen Grab auf – der zweitälteste Fund von Vorfahren unserer eigenen Art *Homo sapiens* in Deutschland. Und die beiden waren keine zufälligen Besucher: Praktisch ohne Pause war die Region bewohnt. Dann sorgte Rom für Durcheinander: Gaius Julius Cäsar schickte die eingesessenen Germanenstämme zurück über den Rhein nach Osten und gab das Land den Rom ergebenen Ubiern, die in der Gegend um das Bonner Münster und die Universität ein Dorf anlegten.
Als dann der göttliche Augustus sich kurz vor der Zeitenwende vornahm, die Nordostgrenze seines Reiches mit Befestigungen zu sichern, marschierten römische Legionäre im späteren Bonn ein und gründeten ein Heerlager.

an atlas for people to discover the attractiveness of this region long ago. The first humans are known to have enjoyed this varied location as much as 14,000 years ago. Among them were a 50-year-old man and a woman scarcely half his age, about whose relationship some people still engage in vicious gossip thousands of years later. In any case, this unequal couple and their dog were found in a joint grave in 1914 in a quarry in Oberkassel on the right bank of the Rhine. That was the second-earliest find in Germany of ancestors of our own species *Homo sapiens*. Moreover, the two were not casual visitors – this region was inhabited virtually uninterruptedly. Then Rome caused an upheaval. Gaius Julius Caesar sent the established Germanic tribes back eastward across the Rhine and gave the land to the Ubii, who were loyal to Rome and who built a village in the area around the Bonn Minster and the University.
When shortly before the Common Era the divine Augustus decided to secure the northeast border of his empire with fortifications, Roman legionaries marched into what was later Bonn and established an army camp in an area in the north of the city which is still called Castell.

Vom Heerlager zur UN-Stadt – 2000 Jahre im Zeitraffer

Castell heißt noch heute der Stadtteil im Bonner Norden, wo in Spitzenzeiten bis zu 7000 römische Soldaten eine fast quadratische Festung mit einer Seitenlänge von über einem halben Kilometer und einen Rheinhafen anlegten. Ein nachgebauter Lastkran am Rheinufer, ein Modell des Lagers sowie Funde im hervorragend gestalteten LVR-LandesMuseum des Landschaftsverbands Rheinland in der Collmannstraße erinnern an diese Zeit. Lange glaubte man, nur ein paar Bäcker, Schuster und Händler hätten im Schatten des Militärstützpunkts in der Ubiersiedlung ihr Glück gesucht. Schließlich stellte die nahe römische Provinzhauptstadt *Colonia Claudia Ara Agrippinensium*, das heutige Köln, alles in den Schatten. Umso größer war das Erstaunen, als 2006 bei den Erdarbeiten zum Bau des neuen World Conference Centers im Bundesviertel ganz andere Befunde zutage traten. Hier, einige Kilometer südlich von Köln, war vor allem im 2. Jahrhundert eine blühende Zivilsiedlung herangewachsen. Aufgrund ihrer Größe von rund 80 Hektar, der gefundenen Baureste und nicht zuletzt der riesigen Abfallgruben schätzen Archäologen die Bevölkerungszahl inzwischen auf bis zu 10 000 Einwohner.

From army camp to UN city – Fast forward through 2,000 years

In its heyday, up to 7,000 Roman soldiers built an almost square fort with sides more than half a kilometre long, along with a harbour on the Rhine. A replica crane on the bank of the river, a model of the camp and various finds in the excellently designed LVR-LandesMuseum in Collmannstrasse recall those times. For a long time people believed that only a few bakers, shoemakers and traders had sought their fortunes in the Ubii settlement in the shadow of this military base. After all, the nearby Roman provincial capital *Colonia Claudia Ara Agrippinensium*, present-day Cologne, put everything in the shade. People were all the more amazed when in 2006, during excavation for the new World Conference Center building in the Bundesviertel, the former federal parliament and government district, quite different finds came to light. Here, a few kilometres south of Cologne, a flourishing civilian settlement had grown up, mainly in the second century. Based on its size of around 80 hectares, the building remains found, and not least the gigantic rubbish pit, archaeologists now estimate that it had up to 10,000 inhabitants. So seemingly it was not just a scattering of peasants who left their cottages in the country

Damit waren es wohl nicht nur ein paar versprengte Bauern, die aus ihren Katen auf dem Land in die City gezogen waren. Bonn war fast halb so groß wie das mächtige Köln und damit für antike Verhältnisse eine ziemlich ansehnliche Stadt – wenngleich unklar ist, ob das damalige Bonn über Stadtrechte verfügte. Offenbar ließen sich an der durchlässigen Grenze des Reiches zum Freien Germanien, das gleich jenseits des Rheins begann, glänzende Geschäfte machen. Schließlich hatten beide Parteien zahlreiche Waren, die auf der anderen Seite stark nachgefragt wurden – Glaskunst, Metallwerkzeuge und Waffen, Wein und Öl hier, Holz, Felle und Sklaven dort. In den Fachwerkhäusern warben Geschäfte, Spezialhandwerker wie Glasbläser und Tavernen um Kundschaft. Ein Tempel diente gallorömischen Kulten, ein geräumiges Badehaus der Entspannung und ein mächtiges Monument zum Rhein hin womöglich den Germanen als Hinweis auf die neuen Besitzer.

Gut zwei Jahrhunderte ging das gut. Dann drängten die Franken mit Macht von Osten über den Rhein. Lange stellte man sich das Ende der römischen Welt als filmreifen Untergang vor. Tatsächlich vermischten sich

and moved to the city. Bonn was nearly half as big as mighty Cologne and thus for ancient times a fairly sizeable city, although it is not clear whether it had civic rights in those days. Evidently there was brilliant business to be done on the Empire's porous border with Free Germania, which started right on the opposite side of the Rhine. After all, both parties had numerous goods that were in high demand on the other side – glassware, metal tools and weapons, wine and oil here, timber, furs and slaves there. In the half-timbered buildings, shops, specialist craftsmen such as glass blowers, and taverns vied for customers. A temple served for Gallo-Roman rituals and a spacious bathhouse for relaxation, while a mighty monument facing the Rhine was possibly meant to remind the Germanic peoples of the new owners.

Things went well for a good two hundred years, until the Franks forced their way across the Rhine from the east. For a long time, people thought of the end of the Roman world as a dramatic downfall. In fact, the Roman and Franconian elites gradually mingled. The last known mercenary in the service of Rome in our area was buried in around 400 CE by the army camp's eastern wall. The

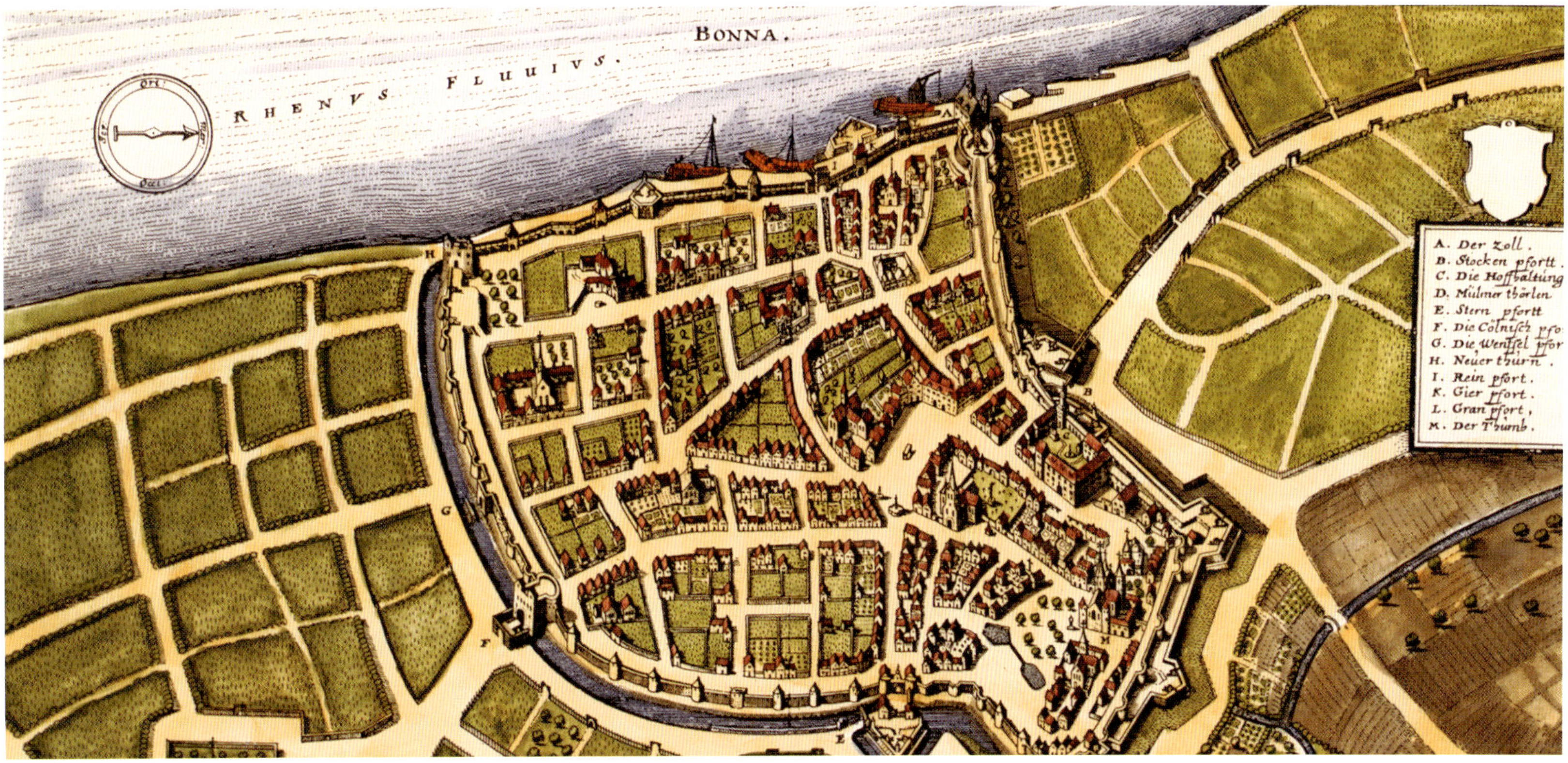

Im Hochmittelalter genehmigten die Bonner Landesherren, die Fürstbischöfe von Köln, der Stadt eine eigene Mauer. Auf dem Kupferstich aus der Werkstatt von Matthaeus Merian dem Älteren (1593–1650) unten ist sie gut zu erkennen. Überreste sind heute noch am Alten Zoll erhalten.

In the High Middle Ages the sovereign lords of Bonn, the Prince Bishops of Cologne, gave the city permission to build its own wall. It is clearly visible on the copperplate engraving below, which originates from the workshop of Matthaeus Merian the Elder, 1593–1650. Some remains of it still survive near the Alter Zoll.

römische und fränkische Eliten nach und nach. Der letzte bekannte Söldner in römischen Diensten wurde in unserer Gegend um 400 n. Chr. an der Ostmauer des Heerlagers begraben. Die ungeschützte zivile Siedlung im Süden gab man auf. Wer blieb, zog lieber in die Nähe der Mauern rund um das heutige Münster. An dessen Stelle entstand dann zwar nicht die erste Kirche der Stadt, aber dort, wo die Römer ihrer Toten gedacht hatten, recycelten die Franken römische Bautrümmer und Schmucksteine, um ihrerseits einen Saal zu Ehren ihrer Verstorbenen zu errichten. Die Gräber darunter boten später Anlass für die christliche Legende, zwei Versprengte der legendären Thebaischen Legion aus dem Osten des Römischen Reiches hätten hier als Opfer der Christenverfolgungen im 3. Jahrhundert ihre letzte Ruhe gefunden. Christliche Missionare erklärten diese beiden, Cassius und Florentius, im 7. Jahrhundert zu Märtyrern und gestalteten die Grabkapelle zum Wallfahrtsort um. Immer am Abend des 10. Oktober öffnet der Stadtdechant, der erste Repräsentant der katholischen Kirche in Bonn, nach einer feierlichen Prozession rund um das Münster die Bronzefalltür über der Gruft

unprotected civilian settlement to the south was abandoned. Those who remained preferred to move close to the walls around the present-day Minster. What was built on this site was not the city's first church. Rather, the Franks recycled Roman building rubble and ornamental stones to build a hall in honour of their own dead on the site where the Romans had remembered theirs. The graves beneath later gave rise to the Christian legend that two legionaries who had separated from the legendary Theban Legion from the eastern Roman Empire had been laid to rest here in the third century as victims of the persecution of Christians. In the seventh century, Christian missionaries pronounced the two, Cassius und Florentius, as martyrs and turned the funerary chapel into a place of pilgrimage. On 10 October each year after a ceremonial procession round the Minster the City Dean, the first representative of the Catholic Church in Bonn, opens the bronze trap door over the crypt for prayers. Bonn owes a great deal to the legend of Cassius and Florentius. The pilgrimage site was not only the nucleus of the Minster basilica later erected above it, but also of the mediaeval city that developed around it.

Die Münsterbasilika aus dem 11. Jahrhundert trägt noch sehr deutlich romanische Züge. Mit ihrem 81 Meter hohen Vierungsturm überragt sie mühelos die meisten anderen Gebäude in der Innenstadt. Und ihre acht Glocken läuten täglich zum Gebet.

The eleventh-century Minster basilica still has clear Romanesque features. With its 81-metre crossing tower, it towers well above most other buildings in the city centre. Moreover, its eight bells sound the call to prayer every day.

Das Kurfürstliche Schloss erstrahlt bis heute wenigstens von außen in barockem Glanz. Hinter seinen Mauern wird seit 200 Jahren gebüffelt. Seit 1818 residiert hier die Rheinische Friedrich-Wilhelms-Universität.

The Electoral Palace still exudes Baroque splendour, at least from outside. Behind its walls, students have swotted for 200 years. Since 1818 it has been the home of Bonn University, the Rheinische Friedrich-Wilhelms-Universität.

zum Gebet. Bonn hat der Legende um Cassius und Florentius viel zu verdanken: Die Pilgerstätte war nicht nur der Kern für die später über dieser Stelle errichtete Münsterbasilika, sondern auch für die sich darum entwickelnde mittelalterliche Stadt. Einen historischen Beleg für das Leben der Bonner Heiligen gibt es nicht. Aber die Stadt erinnert sich dennoch respektvoll an sie und hat ihre überlebensgroßen Granitköpfe deshalb als Skulpturen vor der Münsterapsis platziert.
Als ungebetene Gäste kamen im 9. Jahrhundert Wikinger und Normannen nach Bonn und nahmen sich wiederholt, was sie brauchen konnten. Das tat der erfolgreichen Entwicklung der Stadt allerdings keinen dauerhaften Abbruch. Parallel zum wohlhabenden Stiftsbezirk rund um die Münster-Basilika wuchs auch eine ansehnliche Marktsiedlung heran. Die war für die regierenden Kölner Erzbischöfe so wertvoll, dass sie ihr im Hochmittelalter eine eigene Stadtmauer bis hinab zum Rhein genehmigten. Einen echten Aufschwung nahm die Stadt dann nach 1288. Die reich gewordenen Kölner Patrizier erhoben sich in diesem Jahr militärisch gegen ihren Landesherrn, den Erzbischof und Kölner Kurfürsten

There is no historical evidence of the life of these Bonn saints, but the city remembers them with respect and placed two outsize granite sculptures of their heads in front of the Minster apse.
In the ninth century Vikings and Normans came to Bonn as uninvited guests and repeatedly took what they needed. However, that did no lasting damage to the city's successful development. In parallel with the prosperous monastery district around the Minster basilica, a sizeable market settlement grew up. The ruling Archbishops of Cologne found it so valuable that in the High Middle Ages they allowed it to build its own city wall right down to the Rhine. The city really started to boom in 1288, when Cologne patricians, who had grown rich, staged a military uprising against their ruler, Siegfried von Westerburg, Archbishop and Elector of Cologne. At the Battle of Worringen, they actually expelled him from the city, after which the Archbishop was only allowed to visit his cathedral in Cologne for important church festivals. Bonn became his alternative accommodation. However, the Prince Bishops of the Electorate of Cologne officially acknowledged this fall from grace only in the late

Das Sterntor ist ein Überbleibsel der alten Stadtmauer. Auf Anregung von Kaiser Wilhelm II. wurde es aus deren alten Steinen nach dem Geschmack des 19. Jahrhunderts wieder zusammengefügt, nachdem die Stadtväter die Mauern achtlos hatten schleifen lassen.

The Sterntor is a remnant of the old city wall. After the city fathers had thoughtlessly had the wall razed, on Kaiser Wilhelm II's suggestion some of its stones were reassembled in a style that suited nineteenth-century tastes.

Auf dem Stocktor oder Koblenzer Tor im Kurfürstlichen Schloss (oben links) schwingt der heilige Michael sein Schwert (rechts). Mit der Marktfontaine vor dem Alten Rathaus (unten links) ließ sich 1777 Kurfürst Maximilian Friedrich von Königsegg-Rothenfels bejubeln. Zahlen durften die Bürger.

On the Stocktor or Koblenzer Tor gate in the Electoral Palace (above left), St. Michael wields his sword (right). In 1777, Elector Maximilian Friedrich von Königsegg-Rothenfels commissioned the building of the fountain on the market square in front of the Altes Rathaus in his own honour – at, of course, the townspeople's expense (below left) .

Siegfried von Westerburg, und setzten diesen in der Schlacht von Worringen tatsächlich vor die Tür bzw. vor die Stadttore. Seinen Dom in Köln durfte der Erzbischof fortan nur noch zu hohen kirchlichen Feiertagen besuchen. Bonn wurde zum Ausweichquartier. Zwar machten die Kurkölner Fürstbischöfe ihre Schmach erst im späten 16. Jahrhundert amtlich: 1567 gab Salentin von Isenburg das Kurfürstliche Schloss in Bonn in Auftrag. Drei Jahrzehnte später wurde Bonn offiziell Hauptstadt des Fürstentums. Dennoch profitierte die Stadt schon ab dem 14. Jahrhundert ein halbes Jahrtausend lang von ihrem Residenzstatus. Dass sich aus der Frühphase dieser Epoche kaum Spuren finden, ist allein eine Folge diverser kriegerischer Eroberungen, Plünderungen und Besetzungen, denen Bonn vor allem im Truchsessischen Krieg (1583–1588) gegen Bayern und wenig später im Dreißigjährigen Krieg (1618–1648) ausgesetzt war.

Erst nachdem ein neuer Doppelring mächtiger Bastionen die Stadt halbwegs gesichert hatte, wagte Ferdinand von Bayern ab 1633 den Neubau seiner Residenz. Dieses Kurfürstliche Schloss ist heute vor allem ein Bau des 18. Jahrhunderts, als nach weiteren schweren Belagerun-

sixteenth century. In 1567 Salentin von Isenburg commissioned the building of the Electoral Palace in Bonn. Three decades later, Bonn officially became capital of the principality. From the fourteenth century for half a millennium the city profited from its status as a princely seat. That hardly any traces of the early phase of this epoch exist is due solely to a diverse series of military conquests, lootings and occupations to which Bonn was exposed, primarily in the Truchsessian War (1583–1588) with Bavaria and a little later in the Thirty Years' War (1618–1648).

Only after a new double ring of mighty bastions had more or less secured the town did Ferdinand of Bavaria venture to build a new residence, which was begun in 1633. The present Electoral Palace was built mainly in the eighteenth century. That was when, after further serious sieges, bombardments and the great fire of 1689 in the War of the Palatine Succession, a phase of peace had finally set in. Then, under the absolutist but enlightened Electors Joseph Clemens of Bavaria and Maximilian Franz of Austria, Baroque magnificence was displayed and the electoral capital was enabled to flourish.

gen, Bombardements und dem großen Stadtbrand von 1689 im Pfälzischen Erbfolgekrieg endlich eine Phase der Ruhe und barocken Prachtentfaltung unter den absolutistisch-aufgeklärten Kurfürsten Joseph Clemens von Bayern und Maximilian Franz von Österreich die Residenzstadt aufblühen ließ.
Vonseiten der Bevölkerung hätte es so weitergehen können mit dem Hofleben. Doch französische Revolutionstruppen erzwangen 1794 eine Zeitenwende. Der letzte Kurfürst Maximilian Franz von Österreich, ein Bruder der französischen Königin Marie Antoinette, floh bis nach Leipzig und trat die Stadt wenig später offiziell an Frankreich ab. Das war ein Schock für die Hofgesellschaft und die zahlreichen Intellektuellen und Künstler, die sich im Dunstkreis des üppigen Hoflebens wohlgefühlt hatten. Die meisten zog es fort aus Bonn. Die Stadt schrumpfte und verfiel ins Bedeutungslose. Erst die Preußen, die infolge des Wiener Kongresses 1815 als neue Herren im Rheinland einzogen, hatten ein Einsehen mit der Stadt. Sie ließen die Tradition der 1784 von der Akademie zur Universität erhobenen und 1798 von den Franzosen geschlossenen Universität 1818 wieder

As far as the general population was concerned, courtly life could have continued in this way. But in 1794, revolutionary French troops forced a change of era. The last Elector, Maximilian Franz of Austria, a brother of Queen Marie Antoinette of France, fled to Leipzig and shortly afterwards officially ceded Bonn to France. That was a shock for court society and for the numerous intellectuals and artists who had thrived in the luxurious atmosphere of courtly life. Most left Bonn. The city shrank and declined into insignificance. Not until the Prussians became new rulers of the Rhineland after the Congress of Vienna in 1815 was consideration shown again. In 1818, they revived the tradition of the university, which had been promoted from an academy in 1784 and closed by the French in 1798. Bonn became a centre of academic education in the west, and has remained so to this day with the University of Bonn (Rheinische Friedrich-Wilhelms-Universität) housed in the old Electoral Palace.
Due to the traditionally major role played by Rhineland Catholicism with its conservative values, even in the difficult years after the global economic crisis in the early

Nach dem Zweiten Weltkrieg ragte im Bonner Zentrum die Beethoven-Statue aus dem Schutt (links). Trotz der Zerstörungen (rechts oben) trat 1948 der Parlamentarische Rat in der Stadt zusammen (rechts unten, vorn Konrad Adenauer) und beschloss im Jahr darauf das Grundgesetz.

After World War II, the statue of Beethoven loomed out of the rubble in the centre of Bonn (left). Despite the city's destruction (above right) the Parliamentary Council assembled there in 1948 (below right, with Konrad Adenauer in the foreground) and in 1949 adopted the Basic Law, the German constitution.

aufleben. Bonn wurde ein Zentrum akademischer Bildung im Westen – und ist es mit der Rheinischen Friedrich-Wilhelms-Universität im alten Kurfürstlichen Schloss bis heute.

Die traditionell große Rolle des wertkonservativen rheinischen Katholizismus hatte zur Folge, dass auch in den schwierigen Jahren nach der Weltwirtschaftskrise in den frühen 1930er-Jahren die Nationalsozialisten in der Stadt keine demokratische Mehrheit erlangen konnten. Nur im Kielwasser ihrer reichsweiten Machtübernahme zogen sie auch ins Bonner Rathaus ein. Im Zweiten Weltkrieg büßte die Stadt schwer für Adolf Hitlers Allmachtsfantasien. Hunderte jüdische Bürger und etwa 50 Sinti und Roma wurden Opfer des Rassenwahns. Vor allem beim Luftangriff vom 18. Oktober 1944 wurden Hunderte Einwohner getötet. Insgesamt kamen in Bonn während des Krieges 1500 Zivilisten ums Leben. Im Frühjahr 1945 lag fast das ganze Zentrum in Trümmern. Jede dritte Wohnung war eine Ruine.

Trotzdem hatten gerade repräsentative Gebäude den Luftkrieg erfreulich gut überstanden. Das gab neben der Fürsprache Konrad Adenauers den Ausschlag dafür, dass

1930s the National Socialists were unable to win a democratic majority in Bonn. Only in the wake of their nationwide assumption of power did they move into Bonn City Hall. In the Second World War, Bonn paid heavily for Adolf Hitler's fantasies of omnipotence. Hundreds of Jewish citizens and around 50 Sinti and Roma fell victim to racial fanaticism. Moreover, hundreds of residents were killed in the air raid of 18 October 1944. In all, 1,500 civilians lost their lives in Bonn during World War II. In early 1945 almost the entire city centre lay in ruins. One in three homes had been destroyed.

Nonetheless, some showpiece buildings in particular had survived the air war in pleasingly good condition. That, along with Konrad Adenauer's advocacy, was the crucial factor in prompting the Parliamentary Council to assemble in 1948 among the stuffed animals in the Alexander Koenig Zoological Museum. The following year, Bonn was proclaimed the interim capital of the new Federal Republic.

For Bonn, the 50 years as the German capital were both a blessing and a curse. The population grew. Ministries, embassies and institutions brought work and money.

der Parlamentarische Rat 1948 zwischen den Tierpräparaten im Zoologischen Museum Alexander Koenig zusammentrat. Im Jahr darauf wurde Bonn zur provisorischen Hauptstadt der neuen Bundesrepublik erklärt. Für Bonn waren die 50 Hauptstadtjahre Segen und Fluch zugleich. Die Bevölkerung wuchs. Ministerien, Botschaften und Institutionen brachten Arbeit und Geld. Die Stadt quetschte sich aber mit neuen Großsiedlungen wie Auerberg und Tannenbusch immer enger im Rheintal zusammen. Für Industrie und Gewerbe blieb kaum Platz. In den 1980er-Jahren nahmen Pläne Gestalt an, aus dem Provisorium endlich eine Dauerlösung zu machen. Teil davon war schon vor dem Neubau des Plenarsaals, des Schürmann-Baus für die Abgeordneten und der Museumsmeile auch die „Kanzler-U-Bahn“. Seit Ende der 1970er-Jahre verkehrt sie als Stadtbahn unter der B9 – genau dort, wo 2000 Jahre vorher alles begann. Auch nach dem Umzug des Parlaments und der meisten Ministerien nach Berlin hat sich daran nichts geändert. Und im Langen Eugen, wo früher die Abgeordneten ihre Büros hatten, sitzen jetzt die Vereinten Nationen.

At the same time, with large new settlements such as Auerberg and Tannenbusch, the city crammed itself ever more tightly in the Rhine Valley. There was hardly room for industry and commerce. In the 1980s, plans took shape to turn the provisional solution into a permanent arrangement. The new assembly hall building, the Schürmann Building for members of parliament, and the Museum Mile, along with the underground railway known as the “Chancellor Line,” were visibly part of this. Since the 1970s this municipal railway has run beneath the B9 highway, in exactly the spot where it all began 2,000 years ago. After the German parliament and most federal ministries had moved to Berlin, none of that changed. And the tall building known as Langer Eugen, where parliamentarians had their offices, is now the United Nations campus.

Ludwig van Beethoven (1770–1827) ist zweifelsohne Bonns bekanntester Spross. In der Stadt begegnet man seinem Konterfei deshalb an verschiedensten Stellen, am prominentesten natürlich auf dem Münsterplatz.

Ludwig van Beethoven, 1770–1827, is without a doubt Bonn's most famous son, which is why you come across his effigy in a wide range of places, of which the most prominent is of course the Münsterplatz.

Das Zentrum – Hier schlägt das Herz der Stadt

„Tüte Bananen, einsfuffzich!“, „Frische Tomaten – ein Kilo zwei Euro.“ Auf dem Marktplatz in der Bonner Innenstadt haben die Marktleute ihr vormittägliches Verkaufsritual begonnen. Vor dem Restaurant „Em Höttche“ an der Ecke neben dem Alten Rathaus, wo schon der junge Beethoven auf den Tischen getanzt haben soll, stellt eine Kellnerin Salzstreuer auf die Tische. Wenige Schritte weiter auf dem Münsterplatz sitzen die ersten Gäste zum zweiten Cappuccino vor dem Glaspavillon in der warmen Morgensonne. Eine Reisegruppe steht um das Stadtmodell aus Bronze und lässt sich die Geschichte der Stadtpatrone Cassius und Florentius erklären – und warum das Münster bis vor Kurzem dennoch St. Martin gewidmet war. „Das war der Patron der Pfarrkirche für die Stadtgemeinde. Die stand direkt neben der Münsterbasilika, wie Sie hier vorne an den Umrissen im Straßenpflaster erkennen können. Erst nach ihrem Abriss 1812 durften die einfachen Christen auch ins Münster und nahmen den heiligen Martin dorthin mit“, erklärt die Stadtführerin.

Im Bonner Zentrum hat nur das Knusperhäuschen am Dreieck den großen Stadtbrand von 1689 halbwegs

The centre – Where the heart of the city beats

“Bag of bananas, one fifty!” “Fresh tomatoes, two euros a kilo!” The market traders have begun their morning sales routine on the market square in Bonn city centre. Outside the “Em Höttche” restaurant on the corner next to the Altes Rathaus, where the young Beethoven is said to have danced on the tables, a waitress places salt cellars on the tables. A few steps further on Münsterplatz the first guests are drinking their second cappuccino outside the glass pavilion in the warm morning sunshine. A group of tourists are standing round a bronze model of the city listening to the story of Bonn’s patron saints, Cassius and Florentius, and hearing why until recently the Minster was nevertheless dedicated to St. Martin. “He was the patron saint of the parish church for the town congregation. It was directly next door to the Minster basilica, as you can see from the outlines in the pavement. Only after it was demolished in 1812 were ordinary Christians allowed to enter the Minster, and they took St. Martin with them,” the city guide explains.

In the centre of Bonn, only the building known as the Knusperhäuschen (Gingerbread House) survived the

Die Münsterbasilika dient seit dem 19. Jahrhundert als Pfarrkirche der Stadtgemeinde St. Martin. Im Kreuzgang (rechts oben) fühlt man sich unwillkürlich ins Hohe Mittelalter zurückversetzt. In der Krypta (rechts unten) werden die heiligen Stadtpatrone Cassius und Florentius verehrt.

The Minster basilica has been the parish church of the town congregation of St. Martin since the nineteenth century. In the cloister (above right) you instinctively feel as if you had been transported back into the High Middle Ages. St. Cassius and St. Florentius, the patron saints of Bonn, are venerated in the crypt (below right).

Tische und Stühle stehen vor den zahllosen Kneipen und Cafés in der Innenstadt, so am Friedens- und am Remigiusplatz (Bilder oben). Die Sternstraße (unten links) ist eine attraktive Einkaufsmeile zwischen Markt und Friedensplatz. Die Kirschblüte lockt zur Heerstraße in der Nordstadt (unten rechts).

Tables and chairs stand outside numerous city-centre bars and cafés like these on Friedensplatz and Remigiusplatz (above). Sternstrasse (below left) is an attractive shopping street between Markt and Friedensplatz. The cherry blossom attracts visitors to Heerstrasse in the Nordstadt district (below right).

intakt überstanden und vermittelt einen Eindruck von den beengten Verhältnissen, unter denen das gemeine Volk damals lebte. Dem Zweiten Weltkrieg fiel dann auch ein großer Teil der Folgebauten zum Opfer. Und im Erneuerungseifer der Nachkriegsjahre riss man weitere Gebäuderiegel aus der Zeit des Historismus nieder, um Platz etwa für das Stadthaus oder das Bonner Loch zu schaffen, den Eingang zur U-Bahn vor dem Hauptbahnhof. Einen Eindruck vom Bonn des 19. Jahrhunderts bekommt man deshalb am besten in der Südstadt mit ihren stillen Straßen unter hohen Bäumen, den Stadtvillen und den winzigen Winkbalkonen, von denen aus die vermögenden Bewohner früher gekrönten Häuptern bei der Durchfahrt mit der Eisenbahn huldigen konnten. Auch im Zentrum orientiert sich der Rest des Stadtbildes an den höchstens dreistöckigen Bauten des 19. Jahrhunderts. Stuckornamente, Erker und Giebel sind herausgeputzt – die fußläufige Innenstadt lässt sich in einem Rundkurs bequem durchstreifen. Bonn ist eine Stadt des Schlenderschritts, wo sich rheinische Gemütlichkeit bewusst der Hektik des Großstadttreibens entgegenstellt.

great fire of 1689 more or less intact. It conveys an impression of the cramped conditions in which the common people lived in those days. A large proportion of the next generation of buildings fell victim to World War II, and in the post-war zeal for renewal further rows of Historicist-era buildings were torn down to make way for others such as the Stadthaus (Town Hall) or the Bonner Loch (Bonn Hole), the entrance to the underground railway outside the central station. Consequently, the best place to gain an impression of nineteenth-century Bonn is in the Südstadt with its peaceful streets beneath tall trees, its town villas and tiny balconies from which well-off residents could wave and pay homage to royal personages as they passed through on the train. In the centre, too, the rest of the cityscape is oriented toward nineteenth-century buildings that are at most three storeys high and arrayed with stucco ornaments, bay windows and gables. A circuit of the city centre can easily be made on foot. Bonn is a city for ambling slowly, a city where Rhenish *Gemütlichkeit* consciously confronts the hectic pace of big-city bustle.

Als Rentiers-, Studenten- und Beamtenstadt genoss Bonn im 19. Jahrhundert große Anziehungskraft für wohlhabende Bürger. Entsprechend prächtig fielen deren Neubauten aus, die man heute am Poppelsdorfer Weiher (links) oder in der benachbarten Kurfürstenstraße (Bilder rechts) bewundern kann.

In the nineteenth century, Bonn was a city of students, civil servants and people who lived on private means, and as such a highly attractive location for affluent citizens. Their buildings, examples of which can still be admired at Poppelsdorf Weiher (left) or in neighbouring Kurfürstenstrasse (right), were correspondingly grand.

Vermutlich am 16. Dezember 1770 brachte Maria Magdalena van Beethoven, Gattin eines Tenorsängers am kurfürstlichen Hof, in der Bonngasse ihren Sohn Ludwig zur Welt. Der Knabe blieb 22 Jahre in der Stadt. Dann wurde er in Salzburg und Wien ein Weltstar.

Maria Magdalena van Beethoven, the wife of a tenor singer at the Elector's court, gave birth to her son Ludwig in Bonngasse, probably on 16 December 1770. The boy stayed in the city for 22 years before becoming an international star in Salzburg and Vienna.

Doch auch wenn überall Cafés und vor allem die Hofgartenwiese vor dem alten Kurfürstlichen Schloss zum Pausieren einladen, verdienen einige Bauwerke unterwegs einen genaueren Blick. Vom schmucken Hauptbahnhof aus den 1880er-Jahren, auf dessen Treppe Heinrich Böll 1962 seinen Protagonisten Hans Schnier in den „Ansichten eines Clowns“ den Hut aufhalten ließ, kommt man nach wenigen Gehminuten direkt auf den Münsterplatz. Vor allem die romanische Münsterbasilika aus dem 11. Jahrhundert sticht dort ins Auge. Ihr Vierungsturm ist mit 81 Metern Höhe noch heute die höchste Spitze der Innenstadt. Besonders erbaulich ist die Atmosphäre im Kreuzgang des ehemaligen Stifts dahinter.

Vor dem alten Postamt steht dann auch Bonns bekanntester Sohn auf einem hohen Sockel: Ludwig van Beethoven. Queen Victoria und Preußen-König Friedrich Wilhelm IV. kamen im Sommer 1845 persönlich zur Einweihung dieses Denkmals von Bildhauer Ernst Hähnel. Franz Liszt dirigierte. Seit Erfindung der Fotografie dient die Bronzefigur als Hintergrund für zahlreiche Erinnerungsbilder. Doch damit nicht genug: In

Though ubiquitous cafés and above all the Hofgarten meadow in front of the old Electoral Palace are inviting places to linger, some buildings en route deserve a closer look. From the smart central station built in the 1880s, on the steps of which in 1962 the writer Heinrich Böll made his protagonist Hans Schnier (in “The Clown”) hold out his hat to beg for money, it is only a few minutes’ walk to the Münsterplatz. There, the most eye-catching sight is that of the eleventh-century Minster basilica. Its crossing tower is 81 metres high and still the tallest edifice in the city centre. The atmosphere in the former monastery cloister behind it is especially uplifting.

Outside the Old Post Office Bonn’s best-known son, Ludwig van Beethoven, stands on a high pedestal. Queen Victoria and King Friedrich Wilhelm IV of Prussia came in person in summer 1845 to attend the inauguration of this monument by sculptor Ernst Hähnel. Franz Liszt conducted. Ever since photography was invented this bronze figure has served as a background for numerous souvenir pictures. But that is not all: in Bonn you can find very different versions of the

Bonn kann man das Konterfei des Komponisten an zwölf weiteren Stellen im Stadtgebiet in ganz unterschiedlicher Ausführung entdecken, darunter auf sieben Büsten allein im Garten seines Geburtshauses in der Bonngasse 20, das ohnehin einen Besuch wert ist. Die markantesten Beethoven-Konterfeis schufen hingegen Klaus Kammerichs 1986 mit seinem Betonkopf für den Vorplatz der Beethovenhalle am Rheinufer und Markus Lüpertz 2014 mit seiner Skulptur für den Stadtgarten.

Vom Beethoven-Haus ist es ein kurzer Weg durch die bewegte Sternstraße, an deren Fassaden man noch die Namensschilder der alten Besitzer entdecken kann, zum zentralen Marktplatz. Vor allem das Alte Rathaus im Rokoko-Stil fällt ins Auge, für das Hofbaumeister Michael Leveilly Mitte des 18. Jahrhunderts die Pläne zeichnete. Die Freitreppe gehört zu den berühmtesten Stiegen Deutschlands. Charles de Gaulle, John F. Kennedy und Michail Gorbatschow standen hier und ließen sich feiern. Aber im politisch aufgeheizten Klima der frühen 1970er-Jahre stürmten auch militante Kommunisten hinauf und verwüsteten das Inventar, weil sie

composer's effigy in twelve other sites in the municipal area, including seven busts in the garden of the house where he was born at Bonngasse 20, which is in any case worth a visit. However, the most striking portraits are the one created by Klaus Kammerich in 1986, a concrete head for the square outside the Beethovenhalle concert hall on the bank of the Rhine, and Markus Lüpertz' 2014 sculpture for the Stadtgarten municipal park.

From the Beethoven House it is only a short walk through busy Sternstrasse, on the facades of which you can still spot the nameplates of former proprietors, to the central market square. The most striking building is the Rococo-style Altes Rathaus, the plans for which were drawn up by court architect Michael Leveilly in the mid-eighteenth century. The outside staircase is one of the most famous flights of steps in Germany. Charles de Gaulle, John F. Kennedy and Mikhail Gorbachev stood here to be lauded. However, in the politically charged atmosphere of the early 1970s militant communists also stormed up and laid waste to the contents because they were unwilling to accept a visit from

John F. Kennedy war keineswegs nur „ein Berliner". Am 23. Juni 1963 besuchte der US-Präsident auch die damalige provisorische westdeutsche Hauptstadt Bonn. Auf der Treppe des Alten Rathauses zeigte er sich Tausenden jubelnden Bonnern. Rechts im Bild Bundeskanzler Konrad Adenauer.

John F. Kennedy was by no means only a "Berliner". On 23 June 1963 the US President also visited Bonn, at that time the provisional capital of West Germany. As he stood on the steps of the Altes Rathaus he was cheered by thousands of Bonners. On the right of the picture is Chancellor Konrad Adenauer.

Der Hofgarten hinter dem Kurfürstlichen Residenzschloss lag einst außerhalb der befestigten Stadt. Seit 1818 gehört er der Rheinischen Friedrich-Wilhelms-Universität und verwandelt sich an Sommertagen in eine kostenlose Liegewiese.

The Hofgarten behind the Electoral Palace was once outside the fortified town. Since 1818 it has belonged to the University of Bonn. On summer days it is transformed into a free sunbathing lawn.

einen Besuch des Präsidenten Südvietnams nicht hinnehmen wollten. Heute kommen vor allem Brautpaare hierher. Das Jawort im historischen Kaminzimmer kostet nur 15 Euro extra.

Gleich hinter dem Rathaus erstreckt sich der weitläufige Komplex des alten Kurfürstlichen Schlosses. Die 1818 gegründete Universität hat seither ihren Sitz in den Schlossmauern. Prunkräume gibt es mithin nicht zu sehen. Ein verborgener Traum in Weiß und zartem Gelb ist hingegen die evangelische Schlosskirche aus dem 18. Jahrhundert im Ostflügel der Anlage. Über dem Stockentor, wo früher getadelte Studenten ihre Zeit im Karzer absaßen, zeigt das Ägyptische Museum der Universität seit 2001 rund 3000 Fundstücke aus der Pharaonenzeit. Darunter sind Gefäße, Waffen, Werkzeuge, Papyri, ein kunstvoll bemalter Sarg und drei Porträts alter Ägypter aus verschiedenen Epochen. Auf der Südseite des Schlosses lädt der weitläufige Hofgarten zu einem Sonnenbad oder Spaziergang ein. Am anderen Ende steht das Gebäude des alten anatomischen Instituts, das heute das Akademische Kunstmuseum beherbergt, mit einer bemerkenswert vollständi-

the President of South Vietnam. Now, the principal visitors are bridal couples. A wedding in the historic Kaminzimmer (Fireplace Room) costs only 15 euros extra.

Directly behind the Altes Rathaus lies the extensive complex of the old Electoral Palace. The University, founded in 1818, has been headquartered in the Palace ever since. Consequently, there are no staterooms to be seen. In contrast, the eighteenth-century Protestant Palace Church in the east wing of the complex is a secluded dream in white and delicate yellow. Above the Stockentor gate, where miscreant students served their time in a detention room, is the University's Egyptian Museum, which since 2001 has exhibited around 3,000 objects from the time of the Pharaohs. Among them are vessels, weapons, tools, papyruses, a skilfully painted coffin and three portraits of ancient Egyptians from different epochs. On the south side of the Palace, the spacious Hofgarten is an inviting place to sunbathe or stroll. At the other end is the old anatomical institute building. It now houses the Academic Art Museum, which has a remarkably complete collection of replicas

gen Sammlung von Kopien antiker Skulpturen in einem Ambiente des 19. Jahrhunderts.
Vom Hofgarten aus kann man sowohl Richtung Rhein als auch zum alten Jagdschloss in Poppelsdorf flanieren. Wendet man sich zum Rhein hinunter, kann man den Rundblick vom Alten Zoll, der weithin sichtbaren Rheinbastion der alten Stadtmauer, genießen. Von hier oben führen Treppen hinab zu den Ausflugsschiffen. Am Ufer spaziert man dann nordwärts zur modernen Bonner Oper und der längst unter Denkmalschutz stehenden Beethovenhalle. Nach der Zerstörung des Vorgängerbaus im Zweiten Weltkrieg war die 1959 eröffnete Halle als erster großer Saalbau der jungen Bundesrepublik ein Symbol des Aufbruchs. Von ihrem Vorplatz lohnt sich im Frühjahr unbedingt ein Abstecher in die Bonner Nordstadt mit ihrer inzwischen bundesweit bekannten Kirschblüte. Die Bäume blühen vor allem in der Max- und der Kölnstraße. Oder man spaziert vom Hofgarten gen Osten, an der Kreuzkirche und den Springbrunnen am Kaiserplatz vorbei auf der Poppelsdorfer Allee zum Poppelsdorfer Schloss. Zu dem schiffbaren Kanal, den die Kurfürsten sich im 18. Jahrhun-

of ancient sculptures on show in a nineteenth-century ambience.
From the Hofgarten you can stroll towards the Rhine or to the old hunting palace in Poppelsdorf. Turning down towards the Rhine, you can enjoy the panoramic view from the Alter Zoll (Old Customs House), the Rhine bastion of the old city wall, which is visible from a distance. From up here steps lead down to the excursion boats. You can walk northwards along the riverbank to the modern Bonn Opera House and the Beethovenhalle, which was designated a protected historic monument long ago. Its predecessor was destroyed in World War II. The present concert hall was opened in 1959 and was the first great hall built in the young Federal Republic, as a symbol of new beginnings. In springtime, it is certainly worthwhile making a detour from its forecourt to Bonn's Nordstadt to see the cherry blossom, now famous nationwide. The flowering trees are mainly in Maxstrasse and Kölnstrasse. Alternatively, you can walk eastward from the Hofgarten, passing the Kreuzkirche church and the fountains on Kaiserplatz, to Poppelsdorf Palace on Poppelsdorfer

Als grünes Band verbindet die Poppelsdorfer Allee den Kaiserplatz im Vordergrund mit dem ehemaligen Jagdschloss der Kurfürsten in Poppelsdorf. Heute befindet sich darin unter anderem das sehenswerte Mineralogische Museum der Friedrich-Wilhelms-Universität Bonn.

Poppelsdorfer Allee forms a green ribbon linking Kaiserplatz in the foreground with the Electoral Princes' former hunting lodge in Poppelsdorf. It now houses inter alia Bonn University's Mineralogical Museum, which is well worth a visit.

dert wünschten, hat ihr Staatssäckel damals nicht gereicht. Aber ein ansehnlicher Wassergraben umgibt immerhin das hübsche Bauensemble, in dem neben Instituten der Universität auch deren sehenswerte Mineraliensammlung und der üppig bestückte Botanische Garten untergebracht sind. Wer etwas florale Exotik sucht, wird sie unter Mammutbäumen, Rhododendrenbüschen und zwischen hohen Palmen und Säulenkakteen in den Gewächshäusern sicher finden.

Allee. The state coffers were not full enough to pay for the navigable canal the Electors wanted in the eighteenth century. Nonetheless, a sizeable moat surrounds the attractive architectural ensemble that houses, along with institutes of the university, its interesting collection of minerals, and the lush Botanical Garden. Anyone looking for somewhat exotic plants will surely find them beneath mammoth trees and rhododendron bushes or between tall palms and column cacti in the glasshouses.

Wie eine Landschildkröte von den Galapagosinseln scheint die Beethovenhalle mit ihrem grünen Kupferdach förmlich aus dem Rhein zu kriechen. 1959 nach Plänen von Siegfried Wolske vollendet, gilt sie als einer der bedeutendsten Bauten der jungen Bundesrepublik.

Like a Galapagos Islands tortoise, the Beethovenhalle with its green copper roof seems literally to be crawling out of the Rhine. Designed by Siegfried Wolske and completed in 1959, it is regarded as one of the outstanding buildings of the young Federal Republic.

Das Bundesviertel – Alter Glanz und neuer Nutzen

„Wohl kein anderes Volk als die Deutschen hätte es fertiggebracht, einen Kanzler zu wählen und ihm dann die Hauptstadt vor die Tür zu bringen", schimpfte der Spionage-Autor John le Carré, nachdem er in den frühen 1960er-Jahren einige Zeit als britischer Botschaftsrat in Bonn gearbeitet hatte. Tatsächlich hatte der längst in die Jahre gekommene Konrad Adenauer 1948 keine Lust mehr, seine Rosenzucht in Rhöndorfer Hanglage nur wenige Kilometer südöstlich von Bonn gegen eine Großstadt wie Frankfurt am Main zu tauschen. Doch nach dem NS-Größenwahn war das beschauliche Bonn auch polit-strategisch gesehen eine Idealbesetzung für das neue Deutschland und hat ganz erheblich zur Integration der Bundesrepublik in die westliche Staatengemeinschaft beigetragen. Ein Vierteljahrhundert nach dem Regierungsumzug nach Berlin hat sich die Stadt inzwischen auch mit ihrer neuen Rolle als Bundesstadt und zweitem Regierungssitz gut arrangiert. Die sechs verbliebenen Bundesministerien fallen in den Außenbezirken auf dem Hardtberg im Alltag kaum auf. Doch die Repräsentationsbauten der „Bonner Republik" ziehen bis heute viele Besucher

The Bundesviertel – Former glory and present use

"Perhaps only the Germans, having elected a Chancellor, would have brought their capital city to his door," wrote spy novel author John le Carré, after having worked for a time in the early 1960s as a counsellor in the British embassy in Bonn. It is true that in 1948 Konrad Adenauer, already well on in years, had no desire to swap his rose-growing on a hillside in Rhöndorf just a few kilometres southeast of Bonn for a metropolis such as Frankfurt am Main. Moreover, after the Nazi megalomania tranquil Bonn was an ideal choice for the new Germany in terms of political strategy, and contributed very considerably toward integrating the Federal Republic into the western community of nations. A quarter of a century after the German government moved to Berlin, Bonn has come to terms well with its new role as a federal city and the second seat of government. The six remaining federal ministries in the outlying areas on the Hardtberg are hardly noticeable in everyday life. Yet the prestigious buildings of the "Bonn Republic" still attract many visitors, some with nostalgic memories, while the children of the twenty-first century are amazed to see the old "doll's house capital."

Die weiß getünchte Villa Hammerschmidt mit ihrem ausladenden Garten über dem Rheinufer ist auch nach dem Regierungsumzug der offizielle Dienstsitz des Bundespräsidenten in Bonn. Die Hausherren kommen aber nur noch selten.

Even after the government's relocation to Berlin, white-painted Villa Hammerschmidt with its expansive garden overlooking the Rhine bank is still the German President's official residence in Bonn. The householders rarely visit it now, however.

Drei Jahre vor dem Fall der Mauer hatte der Bundestag den Bau eines neuen Plenarsaals beschlossen. Die Wiedervereinigung fiel dann mitten in die Bauarbeiten. Das Parlament nutzte den Saal mit Unterbrechungen von 1992 bis 2000. Heute ist er Teil des World Conference Center Bonn (WCCB).

Three years before the fall of the Berlin Wall, the German Bundestag resolved to build a new plenary hall. Reunification came while it was still under construction. Parliament used the hall, with interruptions, from 1992 until 2000. It now forms part of the World Conference Center Bonn (WCCB).

an – die einen mit nostalgischen Erinnerungen, die Kinder des 21. Jahrhunderts mit staunendem Blick angesichts der alten Puppenstubenhauptstadt.

Ein guter Startpunkt zur Erkundung ist die U-Bahn-Haltestelle „Museum Koenig“. Im Lichthof des gleichnamigen Museumsbaus, in dem vor einem guten Jahrhundert der Forschungsreisende und Zoologe Alexander Koenig seine umfangreiche Sammlung von Tierpräparaten ausstellte, kam am 1. September 1948 der Parlamentarische Rat zu seiner konstituierenden Sitzung zusammen. Ein Jahr später verabschiedete er das Grundgesetz und Konrad Adenauer bezog im Museumsbau sein erstes Kanzlerbüro. Heute sind die ausgestopften Giraffen im Lichthof wieder unter sich und staksen unbeeindruckt durch die naturgetreue Savannenlandschaft. Ein Besuch lohnt sich.

Gleich gegenüber sieht man das alte Wohnhaus der Zuckerfabrikanten-Familie Koenig, das unter seinem späteren Namen Villa Hammerschmidt Geschichte schrieb. In dem spätklassizistischen weißen Prachtbau über dem Rheinufer residieren seit 1950 die Bundespräsidenten, auch wenn die heutigen Amtsträger nur

A good starting point for exploration is the Museum Koenig underground station. The atrium of the eponymous museum building, where the traveller, explorer and zoologist Alexander Koenig exhibited his extensive collection of stuffed animals a good century ago, was the venue on 1 September 1948 for a constituent assembly of the Parliamentary Council. One year later it adopted the Basic Law, the German constitution, and Konrad Adenauer moved into his first Chancellor’s office in the Museum building. Now, the stuffed giraffes in the atrium keep their own company and stalk unimpressed through the naturalistic savannah landscape. The museum is worth a visit.

Directly opposite you can see the old residence of the Koenig family of sugar manufacturers, which made history under its subsequent name, Villa Hammerschmidt. Since 1950, this magnificent white late-Classicist building above the Rhine bank has been an official residence of the Federal Chancellor, although more recent incumbents have only called by occasionally. The hoisted flag on the roof tells you when someone is at home. The villa next door is still the Federal Chancel-

noch gelegentlich vorbeischauen. Die gehisste Flagge auf dem Dach verrät, wenn jemand zu Hause ist. Die Villa nebenan ist noch heute der Dienstsitz des Bundeskanzlers in Bonn. Als *maison de plaisance* war das schlossartige Palais Schaumburg Bundeskanzler Ludwig Erhard allerdings zu groß und zu verspielt. Im Garten ließ er stattdessen 1963 den vollverglasten Kanzlerbungalow bauen, der bis zum Regierungsumzug als Wohnsitz der Bundeskanzler diente. Über das winzige Schwimmbecken im Atrium hat sich die Öffentlichkeit damals gehörig aufgeregt. Insgesamt zeigt ein Besuch die aus heutiger Sicht fast erschreckende Biederkeit der Amtsträger. Loki Schmidts Teeküche, das braun geflieste Wannenbad von Hannelore Kohl und das karge private Arbeitszimmer der Bundeskanzler sind längst Zeugnisse der Geschichte. Im benachbarten ehemaligen neuen Kanzleramt mit der bekannten Großplastik von Henry Moore im Innenhof wird hingegen noch gearbeitet. Hier hat das Ministerium für wirtschaftliche Zusammenarbeit seinen ersten Dienstsitz. Draußen vor dem Zaun steht der Charakterkopf Konrad Adenauers als Großbronze.

lor's Office in Bonn. Former Chancellor Ludwig Erhard, however, found the grand Palais Schaumburg, a former *maison de plaisance,* too big and fancy. Instead, in 1963 he had a fully glazed bungalow built in the garden, and this served as the Federal Chancellor's residence until the government moved to Berlin. The public at the time had mixed views about the tiny swimming pool in the atrium. Overall, a visit reveals the office-holders' now almost alarming conventionality. Loki Schmidt's kitchenette, Hannelore Kohl's brown-tiled bath, and the Federal Chancellor's sparse private office have long been testimony to history. In contrast, the neighbouring former new Chancellor's Office with the famous large Henry Moore sculpture in the courtyard is still a workplace, now serving as the main office of the Federal Ministry of Economic Cooperation and Development. Outside in front of the fence stands an outsize bronze head with the striking features of Konrad Adenauer.

Turn right before the entrance to Palais Schaumburg and you pass the former Bundesrat building, the Bundeshaus and the new Bundestag assembly hall. This is now part of the World Conference Center Bonn

Der Kopf des ersten Bundeskanzlers Konrad Adenauer (links) steht pikanterweise an der Willy-Brandt-Allee. Die verschlungenen Formen von Henry Moore schmückten das Kanzleramt (rechts unten).

Im Palais Schaumburg nebenan (rechts oben) empfingen die Bundeskanzler ihre Staatsgäste.

Ironically, the head of the first Federal Chancellor Konrad Adenauer stands on Willy-Brandt-Allee. The curved, intertwined shapes of Henry Moore adorned the Federal Chancellor's Office (below right). In Palais Schaumburg next door (above right), Federal Chancellors received their state visitors.

Aus dem Alten Wasserwerk und dem Bundeshaus (Bilder oben) wurde nach dem Parlamentsumzug ein Teil des World Conference Center Bonn. Dessen Neubau beeindruckt mit seinem gläsernen Foyer (unten links). In der Nähe liegt der Schürmann-Bau – heute Heimat der Deutschen Welle (unten rechts).

After the government relocation, the Altes Wasserwerk and the Bundeshaus (above) became a part of the World Conference Center Bonn. This new building has an impressive glass foyer (below left). The nearby Schürmann Building is now home to Deutsche Welle, Germany's public international broadcaster (below right).

Biegt man von der Einfahrt zum Palais Schaumburg nach rechts ab, passiert man das alte Gebäude des Bundesrats, das Bundeshaus und den neuen Plenarsaal des Bundestags. Heute ist er Teil des World Conference Center Bonn (WCCB), das auf der gegenüberliegenden Seite seit 2015 zusätzlich einen neuen großen Saaltrakt mit eindrucksvollem Glasfoyer besitzt. Hier sind vor allem die Vereinten Nationen inzwischen ein häufiger Gast. 37 ihrer Sekretariate und Institutionen sind mittlerweile in Bonn ansässig, darunter herausragend das Weltklimasekretariat. Etwas versteckt hinter dem Plenarsaal liegt das Alte Wasserwerk, ein Parlamentsprovisorium für 364 Sitzungstage. Als die Abgeordneten sich 1986 hier erstmals zusammendrängten, hätte sich niemand träumen lassen, dass nur vier Jahre später an diesem Ort die Entscheidung für die Wiedervereinigung Deutschlands fallen würde.

In der umfangreichen Dauerausstellung im Haus der Geschichte der Bundesrepublik Deutschland an der Willy-Brandt-Allee kann jeder kostenlos seine Erinnerungen an die Zeit ab 1945 auffrischen. Gleich dahinter lohnen das Kunstmuseum Bonn mit seiner großen

(WCCB), which since 2015 has also owned a big new hall tract with an impressive glass foyer on the opposite side. The United Nations is a frequent guest there. Thirty-seven of its secretariats and institutions are now based in Bonn, foremost among them the UN Climate Change Secretariat. Somewhat hidden behind the assembly hall is the Old Waterworks, which served as a temporary parliament venue for 364 days in session. When the members of parliament first crowded together here, nobody dared to dream that only four years later the decision in favour of German reunification would be taken in this place.

Visitors to the extensive permanent exhibition in the House of History of the Federal Republic of Germany on Willy-Brandt-Allee can refresh their memories of the period after 1945 free of charge. Immediately behind it, the Kunstmuseum Bonn (Bonn Museum of Modern Art) with its large collection of contemporary art, and the Bundeskunsthalle with changing exhibitions on art and history are definitely worth a visit. What is more, in the shadow of the three blue cones on the roof of the post-modern Kunsthalle you have a com-

Sammlung zeitgenössischer Kunst und die Bundeskunsthalle mit wechselnden Ausstellungen zu Kunst und Geschichte unbedingt einen Besuch. Im Schatten der drei blauen Kegel auf dem Dach der postmodernen Kunsthalle genießt man außerdem einen einordnenden Blick über das Regierungsviertel hinüber zum ausgedehnten Freizeitpark Rheinaue mit seinen künstlichen Wasserläufen, Schlängelpfaden und dem Japanischen Garten sowie bis zu Bonns heutigen Top-Arbeitgebern Deutsche Post und Telekom.

manding view over the government quarter, across to the extensive Rheinaue Leisure Park with its artificial waterfalls, waterways, winding paths and Japanese Garden, and as far as the headquarters of Bonn's current top employers, Deutsche Post and Telekom.

Moderne Museumsarchitektur sollte der provisorischen Hauptstadt in den 1980er-Jahren mehr internationales Flair verschaffen. Dazu gehören das Kunstmuseum Bonn (links sowie rechts oben) ebenso wie die drei blauen Kegel auf dem begehbaren Dach der Bundeskunsthalle (rechts unten).

In the 1980s, modern museum architecture was intended to give Germany's provisional capital more international flair. The Kunstmuseum Bonn (left and above right) and the three blue cones on the accessible roof of the Bundeskunsthalle (below right) are examples.

Die Rheinaue entstand zur Bundesgartenschau 1979 als 160 Hektar großer Landschaftspark beiderseits des Rheins. Damals kamen mehr als 7,5 Millionen Besucher nach Bonn. Heute ist die Rheinaue zugleich die grüne Lunge der Stadt, ein Rast- und Überwinterungsort für zahlreiche Wasservögel und ein beliebtes Freizeitareal.

The Rheinaue, a 160-hectare landscaped park on both sides of the Rhine, was created for the 1979 Federal Garden Show. At that time, more than 7.5 million visitors came to Bonn. Now, the Rheinaue is the city's "green lung," a place for numerous waterfowl to rest and spend the winter, and a popular recreational area.

Die Deutsche Post DHL Group ist neben der Deutschen Telekom AG der größte Arbeitgeber in Bonn. Ihre Firmenzentrale lässt sich in allen Farben und Formen beleuchten, ob als Weihnachtsbaum oder Narrenkappe im Karneval.

The Deutsche Post DHL Group, along with Deutsche Telekom AG, is Bonn's biggest employer. Its company headquarters can be lit up in any colour and shape, be it a Christmas tree or a Carnival jester's cap.

Auch wenn heute drei Brücken im Stadtgebiet den Rhein überqueren, bringt die Rheinnixe tagsüber noch immer Fußgänger und Radler in wenigen Minuten für kleines Geld von der Innenstadt rüber nach Beuel.

Though three bridges cross the Rhine in the urban area, by day the Rheinnixe still ferries pedestrians and cyclists from the city centre to Beuel in just a few minutes for a modest fare.

Beuel – Die andere Seite von Bonn

Drei große Brücken überspannen in Bonn den Rhein. Doch am schönsten setzt man wie vor 120 Jahren unterhalb der Ersten Fährgasse für einen Obolus mit der Rheinnixe, einer winzigen Fähre für Personen und Fahrräder, über zur sogenannten Schäl Sick, der „schlechten Seite" des Rheins. Von dem negativen Beinamen des rechten Rheinufers sollte man sich nicht abhalten lassen. Vor allem der Stadtteil Beuel – von 1952 bis zu seiner Eingemeindung 1969 eine eigenständige Stadt – hat seinen Charakter bewahrt. Kulturell ist hier mit dem Jungen Theater Bonn, dem Kulturzentrum Brotfabrik und dem bundesweit bekannten Pantheon-Kabarett in der alten Juteweberei ein zweiter Schwerpunkt im Stadtgebiet entstanden. Vor allem genießen die Einwohner spätnachmittags noch Sonnenstunden, wenn Bonn längst im Schatten liegt. Auf der belebten Uferpromenade zwischen Kennedy- und Südbrücke lässt sich das vortrefflich ausleben. Selbst eine Kopie des „Bröckemännche" reckt ihren Allerwertesten heute an der Flutmauer keck in die Sonne. Das Original dieser Skulptur hing eigentlich auf Bonner Seite an der Alten Rheinbrücke. Die Bonner Bürger drückten damit

Beuel – The other side of Bonn

Three large bridges cross the Rhine in Bonn. But, just as 120 years ago, the nicest way to cross to the "bad side" of the Rhine, known as the "Schäl Sick," is to pay a small amount of money and take the Rheinnixe, a tiny ferry for passengers and bicycles, from the bottom of Erste Fährgasse. Do not be put off by the negative nickname of the right bank of the Rhine. The Beuel district, an independent town since 1952 until its incorporation in 1969, has retained its character. It has become a second focus of culture in the municipal area, with the Junges Theater Bonn, the Brotfabrik cultural centre and the Pantheon-Kabarett in the old jute-weaving factory, which has a nationwide reputation. Above all, residents here enjoy hours of sunshine in the late afternoon when Bonn has long lain in the shade. The lively promenade along the river between Kennedybrücke and Südbrücke is an excellent place to enjoy this. On the flood wall there is even a copy of the "Bröckemännche" sculpture cheekily pointing its bottom at the sun. The original sculpture was actually mounted on the Bonn side of the Old Rhine Bridge as an expression of Bonn citizens' displeasure that Beuel people were

ihren Unmut aus, weil die Beueler sich an deren Baukosten nicht beteiligen wollten. Mit der Zerstörung der Alten Rheinbrücke gelangte das Männchen an die Wand einer Kneipe – und eine Kopie kam ans Beueler Ufer.

Auf den Wiesen hinter der Promenade legten im 18. Jahrhundert die Beueler Wäscherinnen ihre Weißwaren zum Bleichen und Trocknen in die Sonne. Das Rheinwasser verlieh Laken und Decken dabei den legendären „Beueler Duft", der weit über das Rheinland hinaus bekannt wurde. Erst die Dampfschiffe verrußten den Wäscherinnen zunehmend das Geschäft. Das mit viel Liebe zusammengestellte Beueler Heimatmuseum in der Wagnergasse 2–4 erzählt ihre Geschichte. Mit Waschzuber und Waschbrett begrüßt eine Wäscherin aus Bronze vor der Tür die Besucher.

Vorzugsweise mit dem Schiff oder Fahrrad lohnt auch ein kleiner Ausflug zu den rheinaufwärts gelegenen Teilen des Stadtbezirks. Wie eine weiße Ritterburg aus dem Märchenland thront die ehemalige Deutschordens-Niederlassung über Ramersdorf. Heute wird das Bauensemble leider von einer lärmenden Schnell-

unwilling to share the building costs. When the Old Rhine Bridge was destroyed the "Bröckemännche" ended up on the wall of a pub – and a copy came to the Beuel bank of the river.

On the meadows behind the promenade, in the eighteenth century Beuel washerwomen used to spread their white laundry in the sun to bleach and dry it. The Rhine water gave sheets and coverlets the legendary "Beuel fragrance," that was known well beyond the Rhineland. Eventually steamships arrived and increasingly spoiled the laundresses' business. The lovingly assembled Beuel local history museum at Wagnergasse 2–4 tells their story. A bronze washerwoman with a tub and washboard welcomes visitors outside the door.

Also worthwhile is a small excursion, preferably by boat or bicycle, to the urban districts further up the Rhine. A former establishment of the Teutonic Order rises in splendour above Ramersdorf like a white knight's castle in a fairy-tale. Sadly, this ensemble of buildings is now almost encircled by a noisy highway. In contrast, by the river a modern idyll prevails. A site on the border between Ramersdorf and Oberkassel where, until the late

Wo sich heute die Kennedybrücke spannt, stand bis zum Zweiten Weltkrieg die erste Rheinbrücke in der Stadt aus dem frühen 20. Jahrhundert.

Unter der Brücke hat eine alte Fähre als China-Schiff umdekoriert für immer festgemacht.

Until World War II, the city's first, early twentieth-century bridge across the Rhine stood where the Kennedybrücke spans the river today. Under the bridge an old ferryboat made over as a Chinese vessel is permanently moored.

Auf der Sonnenseite der Stadt fühlen sich die Beueler, weil ihr Rheinufer noch im Abendlicht glänzt, wenn die Innenstadt bereits im Schatten liegt (links). Im Heimatmuseum Beuel und am kleinen Rheinstrand vor dem Restaurant „Bahnhöfchen" (Bilder rechts) ist der dörfliche Charakter des rechten Ufers erhalten.

Beuel people feel they live on the sunny side of the city because their bank of the Rhine still glows in the evening light when the city centre is already in the shade (left). In the Beuel local history museum and on the beach by the Rhine and the Bahnhöfchen restaurant (right), the village character has been preserved.

straße fast umschlossen. Moderne Idylle herrscht hingegen am Fluss. Wo bis Ende der 1980er-Jahre an der Grenze von Ramersdorf und Oberkassel die Schlote einer Zementfabrik rauchten, ist mit dem Bonner Bogen ein höchst ansehnliches neues Büro- und Freizeitviertel entstanden. Die Universität bezog die alte Direktorenvilla, ein Restaurant die denkmalgeschützte Rohmühle. Daneben öffnete ein Luxushotel mit breiter Freitreppe als Sonnenterrasse. Zusammen mit den Bürobauten in zweiter Reihe flossen weit über 350 Millionen Euro in das Areal. Bis 2016 wurden 4500 Arbeitsplätze geschaffen. Mit dem Rhein-Palais ist ein weiterer Bauabschnitt in Umsetzung und mit dem Bau der S-Bahn-Linie 13 von Oberkassel nach Köln auch eine moderne Verkehrsanbindung vorgesehen. Vielleicht verbindet irgendwann sogar eine Seilbahn das neue IT-Quartier mit dem UN-Campus im Bundesviertel und weiter mit der Universitätsklinik auf dem Venusberg.

1980s, the chimneys of a cement works smoked, is now the Bonner Bogen, a highly attractive new office and leisure quarter. The university moved into the old directors' mansion, and a restaurant into the raw mill, a protected historic monument. Next door, a luxury hotel opened, with a wide outdoor staircase as a sun terrace. Including the office buildings in the second row, well over 350 million euro was invested in the site. By 2016, 4,500 jobs were created. A further building phase, including the Rhein-Palais, is in the process of implementation, as is a modern transport link, the Number 13 suburban train line from Oberkassel to Cologne. One day there will perhaps even be a cable car linking the new IT quarter with the UN campus in the Bundesviertel and, further on, the university hospital on the Venusberg.

Bad Godesberg und Hardtberg – Villen, Wälder, weite Blicke

Für die längste Zeit seiner 2000-jährigen Geschichte wurde Bonn vor allem mit dem Rhein assoziiert. Erst seit 1969 gehört auch das ehemalige Amt Duisdorf zum Stadtgebiet – und mit ihm die linksrheinischen Höhenzüge im Vorland der Eifel. Wer für die Anhöhen des Hochplateaus den Begriff Berge für übertrieben hält, der möge doch von Poppelsdorf aus einmal mit dem Fahrrad hochstrampeln. In vielen, bisweilen steilen Kehren gilt es immerhin einen Anstieg von rund 150 Metern zu bewältigen. Duisdorf überrascht dabei mit einer hübschen Fußgängerzone, dem schmucken Bezirksrathaus Hardtberg und den modernen Bauten der Bundesministerien. Vor allem das Verteidigungsministerium auf der Hardthöhe nimmt noch heute viel Raum ein.

Von Poppelsdorf kommend, erreicht man zunächst rechter Hand den steilen Zuweg zum Kreuzberg mit der weithin sichtbaren weißen Pilgerkirche. Die im feinsten Barock ausgemalte Heilige Stiege auf den letzten Metern ist auch für Nicht-Gläubige den Aufstieg wert. An dieser Stelle fällt die Eifel endgültig zur Kölner Bucht und damit zur Norddeutschen Tiefebene

Bad Godesberg and Hardtberg – Villas, woods, long-distance views

For most of its 2,000-year history, Bonn was associated mainly with the Rhine. The former administrative district of Duisdorf has only been part of the Bonn municipal area since 1969, bringing with it the ridges in the Eifel foothills on the left bank of the Rhine. Anyone who thinks it exaggerated to refer to the these elevations as mountains should just try to pedal up by bicycle from Poppelsdorf. On many, sometimes steep bends you have to cope with a rise of around 150 metres. Duisdorf comes as surprise, with an attractive pedestrian zone, the smart Hardtberg district town hall and modern federal ministry buildings.

Coming from Poppelsdorf, on the right-hand side you first reach the steep path up to the Kreuzberg with its white pilgrimage church, which is visible from afar. On the last few metres, the Heilige Stiege (Holy Stairs) covered in fine Baroque painting makes the ascent worthwhile even for non-believers. At this point the Eifel finally slopes down to the Cologne Lowland and thus to the North German Plain. So, standing in front of the church, visitors have not only Bonn and the Rhine Valley with the Siebengebirge mountains at their feet. On

Auf dem Kreuzberg lädt die Heilige Stiege von Baumeister Balthasar Neumann zur barocken Wallfahrt ein. Oben warten eine Kirche in Weiß und eine fantastische Fernsicht hinab in die Kölner Bucht.

On the Kreuzberg, the architect Balthasar Neumann's Holy Stairs are an invitation to make a Baroque pilgrimage. Awaiting you at the top are a church all in white and a fantastic long-distance view down into the Cologne Lowland.

Der Stadtbezirk Hardtberg hat ein hübsches altes Rathaus vorzuweisen (oben links). Bad Godesberg punktet mit seinem weitläufigen Stadtpark (oben rechts), den Heilquellen wie dem neu gestalteten Draitschbrunnen (unten links) und der Redoute (unten rechts).

The urban district of Hardtberg boasts an attractive pretty old Town Hall (above left). Bad Godesberg scores with its extensive municipal park (above right), its healing springs and redesigned Draitschbrunnen fountain (below left), and the Redoute (below right).

hin ab. Vor der Kirche liegen dem Besucher damit nicht nur Bonn und das Rheintal mit dem Siebengebirge wahrlich zu Füßen. An klaren Tagen grüßen am Horizont auch die Türme des Kölner Doms und der Fernsehturm Colonius in kaum mehr als 25 Kilometern Entfernung.

Weiter geht es zum Venusberg, wo sich in der Nachkriegszeit die Universitätsklinik in den zahlreichen alten Kasernenbauten angesiedelt hat. Das anschließende Wohngebiet mit seinen weiten Blicken und der guten und im Sommer etwas kühleren Luft war zu Zeiten der Bonner Republik aber auch bei der Polit-Prominenz beliebt. Unter anderem Ludwig Erhard, Walter Scheel und Willy Brandt wohnten hier. Viele andere Bonner kommen bevorzugt an Wochenenden hinauf, um am Südhang des Venusbergs im städtischen Wildgehege Waldau die Hirsche und Wildschweine zu füttern. Der Sonntagsspaziergang oder die Mountainbike-Tour lassen sich von hier aus bequem und praktisch ohne Limit in den riesigen Kottenforst ausdehnen, der inzwischen zum Naturpark Rheinland gehört. Schöne Wege führen kilometerweit unter schattigen Eichen,

clear days, the towers of Cologne Cathedral and the Colonius TV tower a little more than 25 kilometres distant greet them from the horizon.

Continuing, you come to the Venusberg, where in the post-war era the university hospital was established in numerous old barrack buildings. The adjacent residential area with its wide views and good air, which is somewhat cooler in summer, was popular with prominent politicians in the days of the Bonn Republic. Among those who lived there were Ludwig Erhard, Walter Scheel and Willy Brandt. Many other Bonners prefer to come up at weekends to feed the deer and wild boar in the Waldau municipal game reserve on the south slope of the Venusberg. From here, you can extend a Sunday walk or mountain bike tour virtually without limit into the gigantic Kottenforst, a forest that is now part of the Rhineland Nature Park. Attractive paths lead for kilometres beneath shady oak, fir and beech trees through to the plateaus above the Ahr Valley.

Back down in the valley, to the south you reach Bad Godesberg. Its most distinctive landmark is the ruin of Godesburg Castle, built in the thirteenth century and

Fichten und Buchen hindurch bis auf die Hochflächen über dem Ahrtal.

Zurück unten im Tal erreicht man im Süden Bad Godesberg. Markantes Wahrzeichen ist vor allem die weithin sichtbare Ruine der Godesburg aus dem 13. Jahrhundert mit ihrem begehbaren Bergfried auf einem alten Vulkankegel mitten im Ort. Sie wurde strategisch geschickt platziert. Das Rheintal läuft hier in einem engen Trichter zusammen und bildet damit die natürliche Grenze zwischen Nieder- und Mittelrhein. Bekannt wurde der heutige Stadtbezirk Bonns vor allem im 19. Jahrhundert als Kurort, Sommerfrische und Alterssitz vieler wohlhabender Bürger. Auch fast 50 Jahre nach seiner damals wenig beliebten Eingemeindung hat Bad Godesberg sich seinen eigenständigen Charakter bewahrt, besitzt eine weitläufige Fußgängerzone, Bahnanschluss und mit den Kammerspielen das eigentliche Bonner Schauspiel.

Vor allem aber der großzügige Stadtpark von 1880 in der Gestaltung eines englischen Landschaftsgartens und das ehemals kurfürstliche, spätklassizistische Ballhaus sind Überbleibsel aus Godesbergs glänzender

still visible from a distance. You can walk round the castle keep, which is on an old volcanic cone in the centre of the town. It was cleverly strategically located. Here, the Rhine Valley flows together in a narrow funnel, forming a natural border between Lower and Middle Rhine. Now an urban district of Bonn, Godesberg made its name primarily in the nineteenth century as a spa, summer resort and place of residence for many wealthy older citizens. Almost 50 years after its then unpopular incorporation, Bad Godesberg has retained its independent character. It has an extensive pedestrianised zone, a rail connection and the Kammerspiele, effectively Bonn's principal theatre.

Above all, however, the generous municipal park established in 1880 on the model of an English landscaped garden and the late-Classicist electoral Ballhaus are remnants of Godesberg's glory days. The future career of the talented Ludwig van Beethoven was decided there in 1792. Joseph Haydn was so delighted with the 22-year-old's performance that he invited Beethoven to study with him in Vienna. Beethoven never returned.

Vor allem der Bergfried der Godesburg ragt weithin sichtbar aus der Talebene heraus. Er schützte einstmals den Ausgang des Rheinischen Schiefergebirges. Heute liegt zu seinen Füßen ein Ausflugslokal.

It is mainly the keep of Godesburg Castle that can be seen from a distance as it towers out of the valley plain. The castle once protected access from the Rhenish Slate Mountains. At its feet now is a restaurant that is a popular destination for excursions.

Gleich am südlichen Ausgang der Stadt beginnen oberhalb von Mehlem die Weinberge. Sie prägen das gesamte Mittelrheintal bis kurz vor Wiesbaden.

The vineyards start above Mehlem right by the city's southern exit. They are a dominant feature of the entire Middle Rhine Valley until just before Wiesbaden.

Epoche. 1792 entschied sich hier der spätere Lebensweg für den talentierten Ludwig van Beethoven. Joseph Haydn war so begeistert vom Vorspiel des 22-Jährigen, dass er ihn zum Unterricht nach Wien einlud. Beethoven kehrte nie zurück.
Auch das Villenviertel zum Rhein hin spiegelt noch immer den alten Glanz in stiller Eleganz zwischen hohen Bäumen. In Hauptstadtzeiten erwarben hier viele Staaten Anwesen für ihre diplomatischen Vertretungen. Inzwischen sind fast alle Gebäude wieder in Privatbesitz. Nur wenige indessen haben einen derart schönen Rheinblick auf das gegenüberliegende Siebengebirge wie die Gäste im traditionsreichen Rheinhotel Dreesen. Kein Wunder, dass dort regelmäßig viele durchreisende Diplomaten und Künstler abstiegen. Und apropos Berge: Von hier aus sieht man auch auf dem gegenüberliegenden Ufer den Ennert als Ausläufer des Siebengebirges. Auch wenn es die Godesberger und Hardtberger ungern hören: Mit knapp 195 Metern über dem Meer ist der Pfaffelsberg auf diesem rechtsrheinischen Höhenzug der höchste Punkt in Bonn.

The exclusive residential area facing the Rhine still exudes its old lustre in discreet elegance between tall trees. In the days when Bonn was the capital, many countries acquired property in this area for their diplomatic missions. Now, nearly all the buildings are back in private ownership. Few now have such a beautiful view of the river and the Siebengebirge on the opposite side as guests in the tradition-steeped Hotel Dreesen on the Rhine. No wonder that many diplomats and artists travelling through stopped off there. And apropos mountains: from here you can also see on the opposite bank the Ennert, a range of foothills of the Siebengebirge. Though Godesberg and Hardtberg people are reluctant to hear it, at just under 195 metres above sea level, the Pfaffelsberg in this hilly ridge on the right bank of the Rhine is the highest point in Bonn.

Jeck und gescheit – So leben die Bonner

Bonn ist eine offene und lebenslustige Stadt. Das Bildungsniveau ist hoch. Mehr als jeder zehnte Einwohner ist schließlich Student. Und aus den Hauptstadtzeiten sind viele Akademiker geblieben, die es nicht mehr nach Berlin gezogen hat. Die international tätigen Großunternehmen mit Sitz in Bonn – allen voran die Deutsche Post und Telekom – und die Vereinten Nationen mit ihren Ablegern locken zudem Menschen aus allen Teilen der Welt an, die etwas bewegen möchten und die zugleich die hohe Lebensqualität zu schätzen wissen. Dazu tragen großzügige Sportanlagen ebenso bei wie rund ein Dutzend Museen, das städtische Opernhaus und mehr als eine Handvoll privater Bühnen.

Spätestens wenn im Karneval an Weiberfastnacht die Wäscherinnen das Beueler Rathaus stürmen, ist an die lästigen Erfordernisse des Alltags ohnehin kaum noch zu denken. 11 000 Einwohner engagieren sich das ganze Jahr in 134 Karnevalsgesellschaften für die tollen Tage. Und wenn die einmal ausgebrochen sind, lässt ein Großteil der Bevölkerung sich mitreißen. Rund 450 000 Besucher zählen die Festausschüsse in der

Crazily and cleverly – How Bonn people live

Bonn is an open and fun-loving city. The educational level is high. After all, more than one in ten inhabitants is a student. Moreover, many academics from its days as a capital stayed behind there rather than move to Berlin. In addition, the multinational corporations headquartered in Bonn, first and foremost Deutsche Post and Telekom, and the United Nations with its various offshoots also attract people from all over the world who are keen to make things happen while simultaneously appreciating the high quality of life. Generous sports facilities contribute toward this, along with around a dozen museums, the municipal opera house and more than a handful of private theatres.

Carnival, certainly by Women's Carnival Day when the washerwomen storm the Rathaus in Beuel, is no time to be thinking of the burdensome demands of everyday life. Eleven thousand residents in 134 carnival societies work all year round on planning the "tolle Tage," that is the crazy days of Carnival. And once they have started, the majority of the population join in and go with the flow. Festival committees in the city and the districts count around 450,000 visitors over the year. The large

Der Rheinische Karneval ist auch in Bonn eine ernsthafte Angelegenheit. Spätestens am Rosenmontag ist fast die gesamte Stadt auf den Beinen. Und wer nicht im Zug mitläuft, der angelt sich ordentlich Kamelle – Süßigkeiten – aus der Luft.

Rhenish Carnival is a serious matter in Bonn. By Carnival Monday at the latest, almost the entire city is on its feet. And for those who do not join in the procession large quantities of sweets are thrown at onlookers.

Stadt und den Bezirken übers Jahr. Dabei sind die großen Umzüge und der Sturm auf die Rathäuser nur die eine Seite der Karnevals-Medaille. Dazu kommen in der Session vom 11.11. bis Aschermittwoch insgesamt rund tausend weitere Veranstaltungen, auf denen allein in Bonn jährlich rund 170 000 Orden und Abzeichen verliehen werden. Schließlich entstand der Karneval als Verballhornung der französischen Revolutionstruppen und später der Preußen mit ihrem Uniform- und Ordens-Kult. Wer so hartnäckig feiert, hat sich seinen Platz im Immateriellen Welterbe der Menschheit redlich verdient; seit 2014 gehört der Rheinische Karneval dazu.

Doch so identitätsstiftend die fünfte Jahreszeit auf viele Einwohner auch wirken mag, rheinische Traditionen finden auch in anderen Lebensbereichen bis heute ihren Ausdruck – und das ganzjährig. Da ist vor allem der Ableger der mittelfränkischen Sprache, der in vielen Familien und Vereinen noch regelmäßig zum Einsatz kommt. Dieses Bönnsch ist mit seinem langen O statt Au, dem langen A und dem fehlenden Endungs-R noch entscheidend gemütlicher als das artverwandte

processions and the storming of the city halls are only one side of the Carnival medal. Altogether, around a thousand other events take place in the session from 11 November to Ash Wednesday. At these events, around 170,000 medals and badges are awarded each year in Bonn alone. After all, Carnival originated as a way of parodying the French revolutionary troops and later the Prussians with their cult of uniforms and medals. A region that celebrates with such determination has earned its place on the UNESCO world heritage list of intangible cultural assets. The Rhineland Carnival was included in 2014.

Although Carnival, the "fifth season," may give many residents such a strong sense of identity, Rhineland traditions still find expression in other areas of life, and do so all year round. Above all, there is the offshoot of the Middle Franconian dialect that is still in regular use in many families and clubs. Known as Bönnsch, it has a long O instead of Au, a long A and a missing terminal R, which makes it much easier on the ear than the related Kölsch spoken in Cologne. Experienced speakers articulate it devotedly in a melodious singsong voice. New-

Kölsch. Könner artikulieren es hingebungsvoll in einem melodischen Singsang. Zugezogene „Immis" rätseln dagegen oft noch jahrelang, was ihr redseliges Gegenüber zu sagen hat.

Zu einer ur-bönnschen Spezialität hat es dagegen bislang nicht gereicht. Die deftige rheinische Küche, zum Beispiel Sauerbraten mit Mandel- und Rosinensoße, „Himmel un Äd" – Kartoffelpüree und Apfelmus mit gebratener Blutwurst –, Matjesfilets mit Bratkartoffeln und für den kleinen Hunger ein Halver Hahn – ein halbes Brötchen mit Gouda und Zwiebeln –, Reibekuchen mit Kompott oder aber ein Röggelchen – ein doppeltes Roggenbrötchen –, darf jedoch in keinem traditionsreichen Restaurant oder Wirtshaus fehlen. Zum Nachtisch für die Gemütlichkeit dann noch ein Stück fluffige Schwarzwälder Kirschtorte, die dem Vernehmen nach zu Beginn des letzten Jahrhunderts in Wahrheit in Bad Godesberg ersonnen wurde. Und gegen ein Kölsch oder zwei in den Kneipen der Stadt oder den Biergärten am Rhein ist ohnehin nichts zu sagen. Für ein solches obergäriges Bier, das nur im Kölner Raum getrunken wird, ließen selbst katholische Bittgänger bei einer Prozes-

comers, known as "immis," in contrast, often puzzle their brains for years trying to work out what their loquacious opposite number is saying.

As yet, no original Bonn speciality exists. The hearty Rhineland cuisine includes beef pot roast with almond and raisin sauce, "heaven and earth" – that is mashed potato and apple purée with fried blood sausage –, matjes herring fillets with fried potatoes, and by way of light bites a Halver Hahn – half a bread roll with Gouda and onions –, potato fritters with apple compote, or a Röggelchen – a double rye-bread roll – are musts in every traditional restaurant or inn. To be sociable you can follow with a dessert in the form of a piece of fluffy Black Forest gateau with cherries, which by all accounts was actually invented in the early twentieth century in Bad Godesberg. Moreover, there is nothing to be said against drinking a Kölsch beer or two in the city pubs or beer gardens. For the sake of this top-fermented beer, which is only drunk in the Cologne region, Catholic supplicants in a procession in 1850 temporarily abandoned the Saviour on the cross they were carrying behind the door of the Schiefe Ecke pub at Stern-

Das Höhenfeuerwerk zum Volksfest „Rhein in Flammen“ eröffnet seit drei Jahrzehnten am ersten Mai-Wochenende die Bonner Freiluftsaison. Zu sehen ist es von Bord Dutzender Ausflugsschiffe, aus der Bonner Rheinaue und auch vom gegenüberliegenden Oberkasseler Rheinufer.

The Rhine in Flames festival firework display on the first weekend in May has marked the start of Bonn's open-air season for the past three decades. People watch it from on board dozens of pleasure boats, from the Bonn Rheinaue, and from the Oberkassel bank on the opposite side of the Rhine.

sion im Jahr 1850 den gekreuzigten Heiland vorübergehend hinter der Kneipentür an der Schiefen Ecke in der Sternstraße 79 stehen. Seither geht man hier nur noch zum „Gequetschten“.

Ohnehin suchen die Bonner bei fast jeder Gelegenheit nach Anlässen für ein geselliges Beisammensein. Kaum ein Wochenende vergeht, an dem auf dem Markt-, Münster- oder Friedensplatz kein Festzelt oder keine Bühne aufgestellt wird. Das Prachtfeuerwerk „Rhein in Flammen“ lockt Jahr um Jahr Anfang Mai die halbe Stadt in die Rheinauen beiderseits des Flusses. Musikfestivals, Stadtteilfeste, die Stummfilmtage im August, die Großkirmes „Pützchens Markt“ im September, „Bonn leuchtet“ im Oktober und der große Weihnachtsmarkt in der gesamten Fußgängerzone schließen sich an. Und wenn gerade doch einmal nichts los sein sollte, packt der Bonner eben seinen Picknickkorb und zieht auf die Hofgartenwiese oder grillt mit Freunden am Rheinufer.

strasse 79. This hostelry is still called the “Zum Gequetschten,” a reference to the squashed effigy of Christ.

Bonn people are nearly always looking for reasons for social get-togethers. Hardly a weekend passes without a marquee or stage being erected on the market square, Münsterplatz or Friedensplatz. In early May each year “Rhein in Flammen” (Rhine in Flames), a magnificent firework display, attracts half the city to the meadows on either side of the Rhine. Music festivals, neighbourhood festivals, the silent film days in August, the big Pützchens Markt funfair in September, “Bonn leuchtet” in October, when the entire city is illuminated, and the big Christmas market throughout the pedestrian zone all follow. And should there be nothing happening, the Bonner just packs a picnic basket and heads for the Hofgarten meadow or has a barbecue with friends on the bank of the Rhine.

Rheinromantik vor den Toren – Das Bonner Umland

Es ist schon ein Treppenwitz der Geschichte, wie der Süden von Bonn – Out of Mehlem sozusagen, dem letzten Stadtviertel Bonns – zu seinem romantischen Image kam. Während im 18. Jahrhundert noch alle Blaublüter Europas für ihre Grand Tour brav über die Alpen zogen, um in ehrfürchtiger Andacht vor den Ruinen Roms und Neapels zu erstarren und anschließend in den Tavernen die jungen Glieder mit reichlich Wein und amourösen Abenteuern wieder zu ölen, machte ausgerechnet ein Italiener aus Rimini das Rheintal populär. Zwei aus Bonner Sicht glückliche Fügungen kamen dafür zusammen: Zum einen verstand sich der belesene Benediktinermönch Aurelio de' Giorgi Bertola vortrefflich auf die deutsche Sprache, zum anderen war es um seine Gesundheit nicht gut bestellt. So zog Bertola sich erst 30-jährig von seiner Professur in Pavia zurück und begab sich auf Reisen bis nach Düsseldorf. Sein Reiseroman *Viaggio sul Reno* machte 1795 nicht nur den Autor bekannt, sondern auch den Fluss. Lord Byron, William Turner und Victor Hugo folgten und prägten den Mythos einer europäischen Kulturlandschaft.

Rhenish romanticism outside the gates – Bonn's surrounding area

How the south of Bonn beyond Mehlem, its southernmost district, came by its romantic image is an irony of history. In the eighteenth century, while all blue-blooded European aristocrats were dutifully crossing the Alps for their Grand Tour, to stand in reverent devotion before the ruins of Rome and Naples before taking to the taverns to lubricate their young limbs with ample wine and amorous adventures, an Italian from Rimini made the Rhine Valley popular. For Bonn, two lucky coincidences came together. First, the learned Benedictine monk Aurelio de' Giorgi Bertola spoke excellent German. Second, he was not in good health. So at the tender age of 30 Bertola resigned his professorship in Pavia and set out on his travels, which took him to Düsseldorf. His travel book *Viaggio sul Reno,* published in 1795, not only made the writer but also the river famous. Lord Byron, William Turner and Victor Hugo followed him and helped to coin the myth of a European cultural landscape.

The region could not have wished for a better advertisement. As a haven of romantic sagas, lovely countryside and equally good wine, the region soon took centre

Ob als Schüttgut oder im Container – auf dem Rhein werden bis heute Hunderte Millionen Tonnen Waren zwischen der Nordsee und dem Alpenraum transportiert.

Auf der regulierten Bundeswasserstraße ruht der Verkehr nur bei Eisgang oder extremer Trockenheit.

Hundreds of tons of cargo, whether it be bulk goods or containerised, are still transported on the Rhine between the North Sea and the Alps.

Traffic on this regulated federal waterway only comes to a halt in icy or extremely dry conditions.

Vulkane haben südlich von Bonn vor Millionen von Jahren ein perfektes Naherholungsgebiet geschaffen, das, anders als sein Name Siebengebirge vermuten lässt, mit rund 50 bewaldeten Gipfeln, Kuppen und Erhebungen aufwartet.

Millions of years ago, volcanoes created a perfect local recreation area south of Bonn. Rather than the seven mountains that its name Siebengebirge suggests, it has around 50 forested peaks, summits and elevations.

Auf dem Petersberg hoch über Königswinter kamen nach 1945 bevorzugt ausländische Staatsgäste unter. Heute genießt jedermann den Fernblick von der Terrasse des Grand-Hotels.

After 1945, Petersberg high above Königswinter was mainly used as a guesthouse for foreign state visitors. Now, anyone can enjoy the long-distance view from the terrace of this grand hotel.

Eine bessere Werbung hätte sich die Region nicht wünschen können, die sich alsbald als Hort romantischer Sagen, lieblicher Landschaften und ebenfalls guten Weins zum Gegenbild der zunehmend industrialisierten Welt in Szene setzte.

In Bonn hat man ein Hauptmotiv dieser romantischen Entdeckungen fast immer vor Augen. Das Siebengebirge am rechten Rheinufer ist zwar aus kurzsichtigem Widerstand der umliegenden Gemeinden kein Nationalpark geworden und deshalb nur das größte Naturschutzgebiet Nordrhein-Westfalens. Dennoch haben Vulkane südlich von Bonn vor Millionen von Jahren ein perfektes Naherholungsgebiet geschaffen, das, anders als sein Name vermuten lässt, gar mit rund 50 Gipfeln, Kuppen und Erhebungen aufwartet. Passionierte Wanderer können die sieben höchsten auf einer fordernden 32-Kilometer-Tour mit rund 1000 Höhenmetern an einem einzigen Tag erklimmen. In keinem Fall darf man sich aber wenigstens eine der herrlichen Aussichten entgehen lassen: Weniger Geübte nehmen den Kreuzweg oder den Shuttlebus hoch zum Petersberg mit seiner großen Terrasse vor dem ehemaligen Gästehaus

stage as an antithesis to an increasingly industrialised world.

In Bonn one has one of the key motifs of these romantic discoveries almost constantly in view. Because of short-sighted opposition from the surrounding communities, the Siebengebirge on the right bank of the Rhine did not become a national park and is therefore only the largest nature reserve in North Rhine-Westphalia. Nonetheless, millions of years ago volcanoes south of Bonn created there a perfect local recreation area that regardless of its name, which means Seven Mountains, boasts around 50 summits, peaks and elevations. Passionate hikers can climb the seven highest in a single day on a demanding 32-kilometre trek with a cumulative elevation gain of around 1,000 metres. On no account, however, should one miss at least one of the superb views. Less practiced climbers take the Kreuzweg (Way of the Cross) or the shuttle bus up to the Petersberg and the large terrace in front of the former federal government guesthouse. Or you can take the historic rack and pinion railway from Königswinter up to the Drachenfels. It has clattered along since 1883 almost

der Bundesregierung. Oder man steigt in Königswinter in die historische Zahnradbahn hoch zum Drachenfels. Seit 1883 rumpelt die fast unverändert mit einem Stopp auf halber Höhe bergwärts und ist für sich genommen schon ein Erlebnis. Von der neu gestalteten Panorama-Terrasse vor der alten Burgruine liegen einem Bonn und der Niederrhein bis nach Köln zu Füßen. Ob auch Sagenheld Siegfried diesen Ausblick zu würdigen wusste, nachdem er in der Gegend seinen Beinamen erworben hatte, ist nicht bekannt. Ein 15 Meter langes Abbild des sagenhaften Groß-Reptils aus Stein kann jedenfalls zusammen mit lebenden Vertretern der Schuppentiere in der Nibelungenhalle und der benachbarten Felsengrotte besucht werden. Auf der anderen Seite des Gipfels empfiehlt sich der schöne Abstieg durch steile Weinberge hinab nach Rhöndorf, wo man sich anschauen kann, wo Konrad Adenauer in seinem letzten Zuhause auf der eigenen Bahn eine ruhige Boccia-Kugel schob.

Weniger Trubel herrscht dagegen auf dem Weg zum Großen Ölberg. 460 Höhenmeter sind es bis zum Gipfel. Doch der Weg führt durch schattigen Buchenwald

unchanged with one stop halfway up the hill and is an experience in itself. From the remodelled panorama terrace in front of the hilltop castle ruins you have Bonn and the Lower Rhine as far as Cologne at your feet. Whether the legendary hero Siegfried appreciated this view after acquiring his nickname (Dragon-Slayer) in the region is unknown. In any case, you can visit a 15-metre-long stone likeness of the mythical dragon, along with live reptiles, in the Nibelungenhalle and the neighbouring grotto. On the other side of the summit, the recommended way down is a lovely walk through steep vineyards down to Rhöndorf, where you can see Konrad Adenauer's last home, where he rolled a quiet boccia ball on his own court.

There is less hustle and bustle on the path to the Grosser Ölberg. There is a cumulative altitude gain of 460 metres to the summit, but the path runs through a shady beech forest and on the other side can easily be extended to the ruins of the former Cistercian abbey of Heisterbach. The surviving Romanesque apse of the monastery church is used in summer as a backdrop for romantic concerts and still conveys an idea of the

In den Weinbergen von Rhöndorf südlich von Bonn züchtete Konrad Adenauer seine Rosen, als ihn der Bundestag 1949 zum ersten Kanzler der Bundesrepublik Deutschland wählte. Adenauers Haus ist heute eine Gedenkstätte.

Konrad Adenauer was cultivating his roses amidst the vineyards of Rhöndorf south of Bonn when in 1949 the Bundestag elected him as first Chancellor of the Federal Republic of Germany. Adenauer's home is now a historical site dedicated to his memory.

und lässt sich auf der anderen Seite bequem bis zur Ruine der ehemaligen Zisterzienserabtei am Heisterbach verlängern. Die erhaltene romanische Apsis der Klosterkirche dient im Sommer als Kulisse romantischer Konzerte und lässt die einstige Größe des Gesamtgebäudes noch erahnen. Im 13. Jahrhundert in völliger Abgeschiedenheit entstanden, wurde die Kirche damals in der Region nur vom Kölner Dom übertroffen. In der Franzosenzeit landeten ihre Steine schnöde in den Wänden eines Kanals zwischen dem Rhein und Antwerpen. Und der wurde nicht einmal fertig gebaut.

Auch auf der linken Bonner Rheinseite – die Topografie des Flusses als Handelsroute und Siedlungsraum gibt auch die Ausflugsrichtungen weitgehend vor – gilt es einiges zu entdecken. In Brühl – zwischen Bonn und Köln gelegen – richteten sich die Kurfürsten zwei herrliche Residenzen ein. Die Barock- bzw. Rokoko-Schlösser Augustusburg und Falkenlust gehörten bereits in den 1980er-Jahren zu den ersten Welterbestätten Deutschlands. Über eine eindrucksvolle Treppe geht es im Schloss Augustusburg hinauf in die Paradezimmer

former size of the building as a whole. It was built in the thirteenth century in complete isolation, and at that time was second in the region only to Cologne Cathedral. In the days of French rule, its stones landed abjectly in the walls of a canal between the Rhine and Antwerp. And the canal was not even finished.

On the left-hand, Bonn side of the Rhine – the topography of the river as a trading route and settlement area largely dictates the direction of excursions – there is also much to discover. In Brühl, which lies between Bonn and Cologne, the Electors built themselves two splendid residences. The Baroque and Rococo palaces of Augustusburg and Falkenlust were among the first world heritage sites in Germany, having been listed in the 1980s. In Augustusburg Palace, an impressive staircase leads up to the staterooms and into the guard room with its skilfully fashioned imitation marble walls of yellow and green stucco. It is hard to believe that the Wittelsbach Electors held court here for six weeks a year at most, in order to hunt in peace in the surrounding forests. Now at least the premises form a wonderful setting for the popular Brühl Palace concerts.

und in den Gardesaal mit kunstvoll imitierten Marmorwänden aus gelbem und grünem Stuck. Kaum begreiflich, dass die Wittelsbacher Kurfürsten allenfalls für sechs Wochen im Jahr hier Hof hielten, um in den umliegenden Wäldern in Ruhe zu jagen. Heute bilden die Räumlichkeiten immerhin den wunderbaren Rahmen für die beliebten Brühler Schlosskonzerte.

Südlich von Bonn und bereits auf dem Territorium von Rheinland-Pfalz thront der Rolandsbogen hoch über dem Rheinufer. Vor rund 1000 Jahren ließen hier die Kölner Kurfürsten am Südende ihres Einflussgebiets eine Höhenburg als Pendant zur Anlage auf dem Drachenfels errichten. Nach dem Dreißigjährigen Krieg und dem Erdbeben von 1673 blieb nur noch ein letztes Fenster erhalten. Doch dieses wurde als Motiv zahlreicher Gemälde umso populärer und zum steingewordenen Symbol des romantischen Rheins. Um vermögende Passagiere bis an den Fuß dieser legendären Aussicht transportieren zu können, verlängerten die privaten Bonn-Cölner Eisenbahnen 1856 ihre Gleise von Bonn aus bis nach Rolandseck. Otto von Bismarck, Queen Victoria, Friedrich Nietzsche und die Brüder Grimm

South of Bonn and already in Rhineland Palatinate territory, the Rolandsbogen, or Roland's Arch, towers high above the Rhine bank. On this spot around 1,000 years ago the Electors of Cologne had a hilltop fortress built at the southern end of their sphere of influence as a counterpart to the complex on the Drachenfels. After the Thirty Years' War and the 1673 earthquake only a single window survived. As a motif for numerous paintings, this grew all the more popular and became a symbol in stone of the Romantic Rhine. To transport wealthy passengers to the foot of this legendary viewpoint the privately owned Bonn-Cölner railways in 1856 extended their lines from Bonn as far as Rolandseck. Otto von Bismarck, Queen Victoria, Friedrich Nietzsche and the Brothers Grimm were just a few of the people who alighted in the station's splendid reception hall. Now a museum in the station and in an impressive new building behind that was designed by Richard Meier shows mainly abstract art by the Surrealist artists, husband and wife Hans Arp and Sophie Taeuber-Arp. The Bonn gallery owner Johannes Wasmuth, a strong supporter of turning the station into a

Ein Ausflug zu Fuß oder mit der Zahnradbahn hoch zum Drachenfels mit seiner neuen Gipfelterrasse ist für Bonn-Besucher eigentlich Pflichtprogramm (Bilder oben).

Aber auch das Barockschloss Augustusburg in Brühl (Bilder unten) sollte man nicht auslassen.

A hike or a ride on the rack and pinion railway to the top of the Drachenfels and its new summit terrace is a must for visitors to Bonn (pictures above).

But they should also be sure to visit Baroque Augustusburg Palace in Brühl (pictures below).

waren nur einige, die in der prunkvollen Empfangshalle des Bahnhofs ausstiegen. Heute zeigt ein Museum darin und in einem eindrucksvollen Neubau von Richard Meier dahinter vornehmlich abstrakte Kunst des Surrealisten-Ehepaars Hans Arp und Sophie Taeuber-Arp. Der Bonner Galerist Johannes Wasmuth, der sich schon vorher für den Bahnhof als Kulturzentrum stark gemacht hatte, hat einen Großteil der Werke von Arps Witwe geerbt und in eine Stiftung eingebracht. Damit setzt das Museum einen bewussten Kontrapunkt zur Rheinromantik des 18. und 19. Jahrhunderts.

cultural centre, inherited a large proportion of the works from Arp's widow and has put them into a trust. The museum thus introduces a deliberate counterpoint to eighteenth- and nineteenth-century Rhine romanticism.

Bildnachweis, Impressum/
Photo credits, Imprint

Bildnachweis/Photo credits

Fotolia:
6/7, 14/15, 24/25, 28 l.u., 28 r., 37 r.u., 39 l., 39 r.o., 39 r.u., 75, 91

Huber-images, Garmisch-Partenkirchen:
5, 23, 27, 28 l.o., 37 l.o. + l.u. + r.o., 40, 59 r.o. + r.u., 76

Volker Lannert, Bonn:
Cover, 8, 11, 17, 34, 44, 51, 52, 60/61, 62/63, 64, 67, 68 l., 68 r.u., 85, 86/87, 88, 94 r.o., 94 l.u.

Picture alliance, Frankfurt am Main:
21, 31 alle, 36 r.u., 43

Presseamt der Bundesstadt Bonn, Bonn:
Michael Sondermann: 12 alle, 36 l. und r.o., 47, 49, 55 alle, 56 alle, 59 l., 68 r.o., 71, 72 alle, 79, 82

Bibliografische Information der Deutschen Nationalbibliothek
Die Deutsche Nationalbibliothek verzeichnet diese Publikation in der Deutschen Nationalbibliografie; detaillierte bibliografische Daten sind im Internet über http://dnb.d-nb.de abrufbar.

ISBN 978-3-8319-0677-2

Text und Bildunterschriften/Text and captions: Dr. Martin Wein, Bonn
Übersetzung ins Englische/English translation: Mary Tyler, London
Gestaltung/Design: BrücknerAping Büro für Gestaltung GbR, Bremen
Gesamtherstellung/Production: Drukarnia Skleniarz, Kraków

www.ellert-richter.de
www.facebook.com/EllertRichterVerlag